D0549976

Publisher's Acknowledgements

Some of the people who helped bring this book to market include the following:

Editorial and Production

VP Consumer and Technology Publishing Director: Michelle Leete

Associate Director- Book Content Management: Martin Tribe

Executive Commissioning Editor: Birgit Gruber

Associate Publisher: Chris Webb

Publishing Assistant: Ellie Scott

Development Editor: Shena Deuchars

Senior Project Editor: Sara Shlaer

Editorial Manager: Jodi Jensen

Editorial Assistant: Leslie Saxman

Marketing

Senior Marketing Manager: Louise Breinholt

Marketing Executive: Kate Parrett

Composition Services

Compositor: Indianapolis Composition Services

Proof Reader: Susan Hobbs

Indexer: Potomac Indexing, LLC

Series Designer: Patrick Cunningham

About the Author

Kate Shoup has authored more than 20 books and edited scores more, during the course of her career. Recent titles include *Office 2010 Simplified, Teach Yourself Visually Office 2010, Windows 7 Digital Classroom, Teach Yourself Visually Outlook 2007, Office 2007: Top 100 Simplified Tips & Tricks,* and *Internet Visual Quick Tips.* She has also co-written a feature-length screenplay (and starred in the ensuing film) and worked as the Sports Editor for *NUVO Newsweekly.* When not working, Kate loves to ski (she was once nationally ranked), read, ride her motorcycle, and follow the IndyCar circuit – and she plays a mean game of 9-ball. Kate lives in Indianapolis with her daughter, her SO, and their dog.

Author's Acknowledgments

Thanks to all those at Wiley for their support and hard work: Aaron Black, Jade Williams, Scott Tullis, and Shena Deuchars. Thanks to technical editor Vince Averello, who skillfully checked each step and offered valuable input along the way. Thanks to the production team at Wiley for their able efforts in creating such a visual masterpiece. Many thanks and much love to my beautiful and brilliant daughter, Heidi Welsh; to my incredible parents, Barb and Steve Shoup; to my wonderful sister, Jenny Shoup; to my brother-in-law, Jim Plant; to my nephew, Jake Plant; and to mon ti lapin, Francois Dubois.

How to Use This Book

Who Needs This Book

This book is for readers who have never used a laptop. It is also for more computer-literate individuals who want to expand their knowledge.

Chapter Organisation

This book consists of sections, all listed in the book's table of contents. A *section* is a set of steps that show you how to complete a specific computer task.

Each section, usually contained on two facing pages, has an introduction to the task at hand, a set of full-colour screen shots and steps that walk you through the task and a set of tips. This format allows you to quickly look at a topic of interest and learn it instantly.

Chapters group together sections with a common theme. A chapter may also contain pages that give you the background information needed to understand the sections in a chapter.

Using the Mouse

This book uses the following conventions to describe the actions you perform when using the mouse:

Click

Press your left mouse button once. You generally click your mouse on something to select something on the screen.

Double-click

Press your left mouse button twice. Double-clicking something on the computer screen generally opens whatever item you have double-clicked.

Right-click

Press your right mouse button. When you right-click on anything on the computer screen, the program displays a shortcut menu containing commands specific to the selected item.

Click, Drag and Release the Mouse

Move your mouse pointer and hover it over an item on the screen. Press and hold down the left mouse button. Now, move the mouse to where you want to place the item and then release the button. You use this method to move an item from one area of the computer screen to another.

The Conventions in This Book

A number of typographic and layout styles have been used throughout SIMPLY Laptops to distinguish different types of information.

Bold

Bold type represents the names of commands and options that you interact with. Bold type also indicates text and numbers that you must type into a dialog box.

Italics

Italic words introduce a new term, which is then defined.

Numbered Steps

You must perform the instructions in numbered steps in order to successfully complete a section and achieve the final results.

Bulleted Steps

These steps point out various optional features. You do not have to perform these steps; they simply give additional information about a feature.

Indented Text

Indented text tells you what the program does in response to your following a numbered step. For example, if you click a certain menu command, a dialog box may open or a window may open. Indented text may also tell you what the final result is when you follow a set of numbered steps.

Notes

Notes give additional information. They may describe special conditions that may occur during an operation. They may warn you of a situation that you want to avoid – for example, the loss of data. A note may also cross-reference a related area of the book. A cross-reference may guide you to another chapter or to another section within the current chapter.

Icons and Buttons

Icons and buttons are graphical representations within the text. They show you exactly what you need to click to perform a step.

You can easily identify the tips in any section by looking for the tip icon. Tips offer additional information, including hints, warnings and tricks. You can use the tip information to go beyond what you have learned in the steps.

Operating System Differences

The screenshots used in this book were captured using the Windows Vista operating system. The features shown in the tasks may differ slightly if you are using Windows 7, Windows XP or an earlier operating system. For example, the default folder for saving photos in Windows Vista is named "Pictures," whereas the default folder in Windows XP for saving photos is named "My Pictures." The program workspace may also look different based on your monitor resolution setting and your program preferences.

Table of Contents

WORD PROCESSING IN WINDOWS 7 — 100

EXPLORING THE INTERNET AND THE WEB WITH YOUR LAPTOP — 112

13 SECURING YOUR LAPTOP PC 192

CONTENTS

CONTENTS

CHOOSING YOUR LAPTOP PC

Portable computers, generally referred to as *laptops* or *notebooks*, began as a great tool for people who travelled and wanted to bring their computer along. Today, laptops with high-end displays and huge processing power are taking over the desktop, as well.

Although laptop models vary by weight, size, keyboard configuration and more, they share some common traits. For example, on a laptop, the keyboard, pointing device and monitor are built-in.

Like their desktop counterparts, laptop computers run an operating system, most commonly Microsoft Windows. Computers that run Windows are generally referred to as *PCs*, which stands for *personal computers*.

EXPLORE A LAPTOP

Laptop computers are very similar to their desktop counterparts. Both contain a hard drive and other hardware. Both use an operating system, run software and save files. And both can be connected to peripheral devices, such as printers.

Key differences exist, however. For example, laptops, which are designed for portability, are much more compact. In addition, whereas desktops require an external keyboard and mouse, these features along with a monitor are built into laptops (although you can plug in a standard keyboard or mouse if desired). Finally, laptops can run on a battery, whereas desktops require an electrical outlet.

Ⓐ Monitor

The monitor on a laptop is typically made of a soft-to-the-touch, and somewhat fragile, liquid crystal display.

Ⓑ Keyboard

Keyboard configurations vary based on the size of the laptop, with larger laptops having a separate number pad and smaller ones embedding number-pad functionality within the regular keys.

Ⓒ Touchpad Pointing Device

Laptops feature a built-in pointing device – usually a touchpad, as shown here. You move your finger over the pad to move the mouse pointer on your screen.

Ⓓ Function Keys

Most laptops preassign functions to these aptly named function keys. Typical uses are for muting the speakers or accessing the Internet.

E DVD Drive

Most laptops include a DVD drive, although some still feature a CD drive. The location of these drives varies by model.

F Battery

A battery usually slots into the bottom of a laptop. The battery needs to be recharged on a regular basis.

G Power-Cord Connector

To recharge your battery, you plug your laptop into a power socket using this power-cord connector.

EXPLORE SLOTS AND PORTS

You can use the various slots and ports built into your laptop to connect peripheral devices to it, such as a printer, a mouse, a keyboard, an extra monitor, headphones, a microphone, a digital camera and more. Most of these slots and ports are located on the sides or back of the chassis.

Note that, in addition to using the slots and ports built into your laptop to connect peripheral devices, you can also connect these devices to ports and slots in a docking station. You can then plug your laptop into the docking station to access the peripheral devices.

USB Port

You can use a universal serial bus (USB) port to connect a wide variety of devices, from a flash drive for data storage to a printer or digital camera. Devices that can be connected via USB are generally plug-and-play – that is, you need not restart your computer to use them after connecting them via a USB cable. Windows can automatically install many USB devices when you connect them, requiring no additional input from you.

Memory Card Reader

A memory card is a small, removable digital storage device used in many electronic gadgets such as digital cameras, MP3 players and so on. Many laptops feature memory card readers – small slots into which you can insert a memory card. You can then view the contents of the memory card and even use the memory card as an external storage device to save data from your laptop.

Monitor Port

Some laptop computers include a monitor port. If you want to connect an external monitor to your laptop – for example, to show a presentation on a larger screen or if you use a dual-monitor system in your workflow – you can connect a standard monitor cable to the laptop's monitor port.

Ethernet Jack

You use an Ethernet jack to connect your computer to a router that controls your local area network (LAN) through a coaxial or fibre-optic cable. You can also use an Ethernet jack to establish a high-speed connection to the Internet. You simply plug the Ethernet cable into the Ethernet jack on your laptop and then connect the other end of the cable to a high-speed modem.

Modem Jack

Although most people use an Ethernet cable or a wireless signal to access the Internet, there may be times when you must use a phone line. If you need to use a phone line to dial up your Internet connection, you can plug a phone cable into the modem jack to pick up a signal.

PC Card Slot

The Personal Computer Memory Card International Association (PCMCIA), a group of industry-leading companies, defined and developed a standard for PCMCIA (or PC) cards. A PC card was originally a type of storage card but it has expanded to house other devices, such as network cards and modems. Many laptops include slots for PC cards.

Headphone and Microphone Jacks

If you want to use headphones to listen to music from your computer, you plug them into the headphone jack. You can also use this jack to plug in computer speakers. You use the microphone jack to plug in a microphone. You might use a microphone, for example, to communicate with others using a video-chat application.

CHOOSE A MONITOR SIZE

Laptop displays range in size from 5 inches – perfect for portability – to 17 or even 20 inches. These larger monitors are ideal for handling graphics and animations. In addition to varying in size, laptop monitors can also vary in image quality.

Which monitor is right for you depends on how many hours you will spend in front of it and what functions you need to perform. When choosing a monitor, you should keep both size and image quality in mind.

Note that laptop monitors are notoriously fragile. Avoid scratching them or submitting them to extreme temperatures.

Display Size

If you mainly need to check e-mail or type a few memos on the road, a smaller monitor might be adequate. However, if you spend hours reading reports, studying graphs and viewing high-end graphics, a larger monitor is best. Of course, monitor size affects portability, with larger monitors best suited for stay-at-home laptops.

Display Quality

Laptop monitors vary widely in quality. When researching laptop monitors, you will hear various terms, such as "backlit" and "reflective", "active matrix" and "passive matrix" and "TFT". Generally speaking, TFT, active-matrix, backlit displays are superior. A monitor's screen resolution indicates the number of pixels that form an image on the screen; the higher the numbers are, the crisper the display. Look for a screen resolution of at least 1024 × 768 pixels – higher if you use graphics-intensive applications.

Tablet PCs

Tablet PCs are a special type of laptop. Most tablet PCs look more like legal pads than laptops; instead of using a keyboard and pointing device to input data, you write directly on the tablet PC's monitor using a stylus – that is, an electromagnetic pen that sends a digital signal through the screen. What you write on the monitor can be converted to a regular font for improved readability.

If you run into a problem with Windows 7 or you are not sure how to perform a task, try the Windows Help and Support Center. Click the Start button, click Help and Support. Type a keyword or phrase in the Search box. Click the Search Help button ([🔎]) or press Enter. Click a link that looks relevant.

8

CHOOSE THE RIGHT WEIGHT

Laptops started out as portable computing devices for people who travelled regularly. Today, you can find ultra-portable laptops that weigh as little as two pounds. These laptops offer a smaller display and keyboard size and have the advantage of a longer battery life.

You can also buy laptops that weigh as much as 18 pounds. These larger models often include multimedia features and larger screen sizes. In fact, these models are so fully featured, many people have adopted them for use in lieu of a desktop computer.

Choosing the right weight for your laptop involves weighing portability against performance.

Portability

If you need a laptop for use while on the road, consider a lighter-weight model. Be aware, however, that there can be a trade-off in features and price when you buy a very lightweight laptop. A two-pound laptop may be more expensive and less able to handle larger programs or run at faster speeds. In contrast, a larger portable laptop may offer more speed or features, but it may be difficult to carry on long trips.

Stay-at-Home Laptops

Some people use laptops at home in lieu of a desktop computer. Even larger laptops, which boast 17- or even 20-inch screens, take up less space than a computer tower and plugging external devices into them is easier than having to crawl around on the floor or move a heavy tower. With wireless Internet connections and a built-in keyboard and pointing device, they tend to reduce the clutter of cables that come with standard desktop models. Although weight is less of an issue for stay-at-home laptops, consider whether you might want to carry such a computer from room to room or out of the house before you choose the heaviest model.

Rugged Laptops

Some laptops are marketed for their durability. If you work in an industry such as construction, the military, law enforcement, archaeology or any other industry in which your laptop may be subjected to a harsh physical environment in which heat, humidity, altitude or depth may be a factor, one of these rugged laptops may be for you. Water- and shock-proof, their keyboards are sealed to prevent water damage and they can withstand more variation in temperature, as well as the effects of shock, vibration, falls, grease, water and fire. They can also function near electromagnetic transmissions, such as from power generators. Not surprisingly, these rugged laptops are somewhat heavier than traditional models.

DETERMINE MEMORY AND STORAGE NEEDS

Your computer needs a certain amount of random access memory (RAM) to run programs and load files. More RAM can also help your computer run faster. Your laptop can read from and write to RAM more quickly than to other types of computer storage.

Your computer needs to be able to store data. You store data on a hard drive. In addition, you can store data on external storage media, such as CDs, DVDs, flash drives and external hard drives. You learn more about these types of external storage media in the next task.

RAM

The more RAM your system has, the faster items load on your computer. RAM exists on an integrated circuit memory chip, which is rated by its maximum clock rate (how quickly it can request data to appear), measured in megahertz (MHz), and its size, measured in megabytes (MB) or gigabytes (GB). RAM comes in several varieties, including static RAM (SRAM), dynamic RAM (DRAM), synchronous dynamic RAM (SDRAM) and double data rate SDRAM (DDR SDRAM). Note that you may be able to add RAM to your system if it is running too slowly. Doing so involves opening a panel on the bottom of the machine to access the motherboard.

Hard Drive Capacity

Hard drives have a certain capacity for storing data, measured in gigabytes (GB) or, in recent years, terabytes (TB). When you create or save a file on your laptop, the file is saved to your hard drive. You should buy a hard drive with enough capacity to handle your day-to-day data storage needs. Today, a 100GB hard drive is pretty much the minimum standard. The more files you need to store and the more programs you need to run, the larger-capacity hard drive you should get. Hard drives with a faster rotational speed can be useful for power users, enabling quicker access to files.

The Windows Experience Index

Windows 7 supports the use of the Windows Experience Index, which evaluates components on a PC, including the memory, to determine how well that PC will perform running Windows 7. This evaluation is expressed in a measurement called a *base score*. The base score is derived from the lowest of the sub scores – that is, the scores of each component evaluated. Scores range from 1.0 to 7.9.

Basic Requirements

Windows 7 requires a minimum Windows Experience Index rating of 1.0 to operate – that is, 1GB of system memory (RAM) for the 32-bit version of the operating system and 2GB of system memory (RAM) for the 64-bit version. Windows 7 also requires 20GB of available space on the hard drive. In reality, however, minimum requirements for operating systems are not adequate for a smooth computing experience. If you are purchasing a new laptop, you should opt for one with additional RAM and hard-drive space; how much more RAM and hard-drive space you need depends on how you plan to use your laptop.

Everyday Use

If you plan to use your laptop on a day-to-day basis and if it fits in your budget, you should look for a PC with a Windows Experience Index rating of at least 2.0 and preferably 3.0. Bumping up your RAM to 3GB helps to ensure your PC does not get bogged down. In addition, you may want to opt for a larger hard drive – say, 200GB – especially if you want to store a significant number of photos, songs or videos on your PC.

Power Users

You may need to run several programs at once (called *multitasking*). For example, you may want to check your e-mail while running a PowerPoint presentation and opening a Word document. In this case, opt for a laptop with a Windows Experience Index rating of at least 3.0 and preferably 4.0. In addition, you may want more memory – 4GB should do the trick. And you will almost certainly want a larger hard drive.

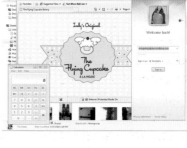

Graphics and Gaming

For the graphics professional or hard-core gamer, a Windows Experience Index rating of at least 5.0 ensures that any high-end games or graphics applications run without a hitch. And again, you will want yet more memory and an even larger hard drive than a power user would require – 5GB of RAM and a 500GB hard drive should suffice.

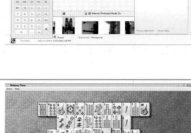

UNDERSTAND DRIVES AND DATA STORAGE

Laptops store data on an internal hard drive – a spinning hard disk inside the laptop chassis – via magnetic recording. An arm with a magnetic head moves over the disk to read or write data on the disk as it spins. Data can also be erased, although the magnetic data pattern may remain on the drive after you have erased it.

Most laptops also have a disc drive. Depending on the type of drive, you can insert a CD, DVD or Blu-ray disc into it to store data on the disc. Other data-storage options include Flash drives and portable external hard drives.

How Data Is Stored

Data is stored in files as a series of bytes in a sector on your hard drive. Each sector on the drive can contain a certain number of bytes. When you access data, whether by opening a piece of software or opening a file, the read/write heads move across the hard drive, looking for the required bytes. These bytes may be located in various sectors of the drive. Bytes in files spread across multiple sectors are said to be *fragmented*; fragmented files take longer to load than files whose bytes are stored in a single segment.

Partitions

You can create partitions on a hard drive that essentially break it up into two or more hard drives. You may do this to run different operating systems on the same computer. You may also create a partition to foster the appearance of having multiple hard drives for file-management purposes or to accommodate multiple users. Creating additional partitions also enables you to separate your data from your operating system; that way, in the event your operating system is damaged, your data remains safe. To partition a hard drive in Windows 7, there must be either unallocated disk space or free space on the hard drive.

Using the Disc Drive

As mentioned, most laptops include a disc drive, into which you can insert various storage media. These storage media include compact discs (CDs), digital versatile discs (DVDs) and Blu-ray discs. Depending on your disc drive's setup, you may be able to read data on and write data to all three of these types of storage media.

Storing Data on CD

Nearly all disc drives support the use of CDs – hard plastic disks on which you can store data, music or images. CDs can typically store up to 700MB of data. To read from or write to a CD, your laptop must have a CD drive with the appropriate support (read, write or read/write).

Storing Data on DVD

DVDs are similar to CDs, but with more storage capacity. A single-layer DVD can store 4.7GB of data and a dual-layer DVD can store twice that. DVDs come in several formats, including DVD+, DVD− and DVD+/−. DVDs also come in readable, writeable and read/write format. Your laptop's disc drive must explicitly support a specific DVD format for you to be able to use that type of DVD.

Storing Data on Blu-ray

The name Blu-ray stems from the blue-violet laser used to read and write to this type of disc. A single-layer Blu-ray disc can store 25GB of data, more than five times the storage capacity of a standard DVD disc and a double-layer disc can store twice that. This storage format, designed to enable the recording, playback and rewriting of high-definition video, is expected to supersede the DVD format.

Flash Drive

A flash drive, also referred to as a USB stick or pen drive, is the size of a pack of chewing gum but can hold a huge amount of data. Plugging a flash drive into a USB port is like adding a second hard drive. Flash drives come with differing amounts of storage space, from 64MB to 256GB.

External Hard Drive

If you need to store large amounts of data – for example, to back up your system – you can buy an external hard drive. External hard drives have storage capacities of many gigabytes or even terabytes. An external hard drive can be connected to your laptop via its FireWire or USB port.

SELECT A MICROPROCESSOR

Choosing a microprocessor, often referred to as a *processor*, is an important part of deciding which laptop is right for you. The type of microprocessor found in a laptop can make a big difference in its performance.

A microprocessor incorporates most or all of the functions of a computer's central processing unit (CPU). The microprocessor is the brain of a computer, enabling it to perform calculations and process data.

The various companies that manufacture microprocessors are constantly working to improve them. Newer microprocessors offer more processing power, handle multiple tasks concurrently, generate less heat and require less power to operate.

What a Microprocessor Does

A microprocessor acts as the brain of the computer, handling data, performing calculations, carrying out stored instructions and so on. Microprocessors, which are integrated circuits composed of millions of transistors, can perform many instructions per second, such as mathematical equations, calibrations, data storage, display updates and so on. A microprocessor is housed on a tiny silicon wafer base or chip, where some or all of the functions of a computer's central processing unit (CPU) are integrated.

Microprocessor Design

A microprocessor incorporates functions of the CPU onto an integrated circuit, also called a *chip*. An integrated circuit is a tiny electronic circuit composed of millions of transistors situated on a silicon wafer. This circuit consists mainly of semiconductor devices – that is, components that make use of the electronic properties of various semiconductor materials (primarily silicon).

Brands of Microprocessor

The two top manufacturers of microprocessors are Intel Corporation and AMD Inc. Intel, founded in 1968, produced the first microprocessor in 1971 – a four-bit processor called the Intel 4004. AMD, short for Advanced Micro Devices, launched in 1969 as a producer of logic chips. In addition to manufacturing microprocessors, both companies also produce motherboard chipsets, network interface controllers and integrated circuits, flash memory, graphic chips and other devices for computing and communications. Chips are constantly being improved to include more processing power, handle more tasks concurrently and generate less heat.

The x86 ISA

Both Intel and AMD produce processors based on the x86 instruction set architecture. The instruction set architecture, sometimes called simply the *instruction set* or the *ISA*, is the portion of the computer architecture that pertains to programming. It includes the *opcodes*, the machine language that specifies the commands used by a particular processor. x86 refers to a family of ISAs spawned by the Intel 8086 chip, launched in 1978 and to the early successors of that chip, which also had names ending in 86.

Clock Rate

The higher the clock rate, the faster your computer can operate. You will often see a clock rate, also known as clock speed, expressed in gigahertz, to reflect how quickly the processor in your laptop can complete a clock cycle or tick. A clock cycle is the smallest unit of time a device recognises, although a microprocessor may execute several instructions in a single clock cycle. It can be useful to compare clock rates of processors in the same family; the faster the clock rate, the more instructions the microprocessor can execute per second. Using clock rates to compare processors from different families can be misleading, however, because the amount of work that different microprocessors can do in a single clock cycle varies.

Dual-Core Processors

Older laptops featured single-core processors. That is, the silicon wafer or chip, on which the processor was housed contained only a single processor. In time, however, computer requirements exceeded the capabilities of these processors. That led to the development of dual-core processors – essentially, two processors on a single chip. Just as two heads are better than one, dual-core processors enable computers to more efficiently start and run several operations at once, at fast processing speeds (measured in GHz) and with lower power usage. Recent years have seen the development of quad-core processors, which are even more efficient than their dual-core counterparts.

Moore's Law

Moore's law, named for Intel co-founder Gordon Moore and coined in 1970 by Caltech professor Carver Mead, describes a long-term trend in computing in which the number of transistors that can be placed cheaply on an integrated circuit has roughly doubled every two years. Gordon Moore observed this trend in a 1965 paper, in which he noted that the number of components on integrated circuits had doubled each year since the 1958 invention of the integrated circuit. Moore went on to posit that this trend would continue "for at least 10 years". The result of this trend, which is in fact expected to continue until at least 2015, has been the increased use and demand for digital electronic devices worldwide.

Choose a Microprocessor

The microprocessor you choose depends on how you plan to use your laptop. For example, if you are a power user or you plan to use your laptops to play games, then you will want a more robust microprocessor. In addition, if you plan to travel frequently, battery life is a consideration. In that case, you might opt for a dual-core processor designed for mobile computing, such as the AMD Turion 64 X2 or the Intel Core Duo processor. These use less power while still providing the advantages of a dual processor. Whichever microprocessor you choose, look for a clock rate of at least 1 GHz.

REVIEW GRAPHICS CAPABILITIES

The graphics card is a circuit board inside your laptop that controls what appears on your laptop's monitor. The graphics card is also called the video card, video adapter, display adapter, graphics-accelerator card or graphics processing unit. The graphics card is particularly important when playing games or running animations.

Laptops that can handle the graphics and animations that appear in many computer games tend to have powerful graphics cards, large screens with a high resolution, a lot of memory and fast processors. They come with a high price tag but, for a dedicated gamer or multimedia designer, they may be worth it.

Graphics Cards

Graphics cards contain a graphics processing unit (a GPU) with a specific speed and amount of memory. For most users, the graphics card that comes installed on a laptop is sufficient. For users who intend to use their laptop for graphics-rich applications such as design or animation software or games, a graphics card with more speed and memory may be required.

Considerations

If you are a hard-core gamer or plan to use your laptop to handle 3-D graphics work, a top-of-the-line graphics card is a must. However, it is not necessary to have a high-end graphics card on a laptop that will be used primarily for such tasks as checking e-mail or using a word-processing program. Note that your graphics card must be a good match for your CPU. A very powerful graphics card with a slower or older CPU would be a waste. Also, be aware that not all graphics cards work on all computers. Finally, be sure to check the frame rate – that is, the frequency at which the card produces unique consecutive images, called *frames* – because lower rates can slow down video and animations.

Brands of Graphics Cards

Three manufacturers of graphics cards dominate the market: Intel, AMD and NVIDIA. Intel owns the low-end category, offering a line of graphics cards integrated into the manufacturer's motherboard chipsets. Although this can reduce cost, power consumption and noise, performance takes a hit because both the graphics card and the CPU share use of the laptop's main memory. If you plan to use your laptop primarily to check e-mail or work with a word-processing program, this type of graphics card should be adequate. If, however, you plan to use your laptop for gaming or working with 3-D graphics, an AMD or NVIDIA graphics card may be a better choice. These manufacturers offer graphics cards that span from the low end to the very high end.

EXPLORE WIRELESS CAPABILITIES

With wireless technology, you can use your laptop to connect to the Internet using a wireless network – without cable connections or a phone line. These wireless networks exist in many locations, including hotels, airports, libraries, schools, businesses, cafés and more. If you plan to take your laptop on the road, the ability to connect to a wireless network while travelling or at your destination, can be very important.

When you buy a laptop, you should make sure that it includes the hardware components necessary to use a wireless network. You will quickly find that a laptop without this capability is much less useful than one that has it!

How Wireless Works

A special piece of equipment called a *wireless router* broadcasts a radio-based signal, which is received by computers in the router's vicinity (assuming those computers have the appropriate hardware installed). Specifically, computers need to have a wireless card installed to access the wireless signal. Computers with the necessary hardware can use the signal for two-way communication. The transmission speed varies depending on the quality of the connection and the quality of the wireless card installed in the laptop.

Wireless Protocols

There are various wireless technology protocols. These include Bluetooth and WiFi, also referred to as 802.11. This technology enables you to connect wirelessly to the Internet. Within the WiFi protocol are several versions, including 802.11a, which operates at 54 megabits per second (Mbps) and has an indoor range of 115 feet; 802.11b, which operates at 11 Mbps but has an indoor range of 125 feet; and 802.11g, which operates at 54 Mbps at an indoor range of 125 feet. In addition, the most recent version, 802.11n, operates at 150 Mbps at an indoor range of 250 feet. 802.11n offers significant increases in data throughput and link range, without requiring additional bandwidth or transmission power.

Finding a Wireless Network

Many restaurants, hotels, airports, libraries, book stores and other public places offer wireless hot spots – that is, areas where you can use your laptop to connect to a wireless router and access the Internet for free or for a fee. In addition, you can subscribe to various wireless services from popular providers such as T-Mobile, Verizon and so on to pick up their signal when you travel.

CHOOSE THE BEST BATTERY

When you take your laptop on the road, it needs to carry its power supply with it – specifically, a rechargeable battery.

The amount of time you can run your laptop on a charged battery is called the *battery life*. Battery life, which varies from laptop to laptop, represents the number of hours your laptop can operate on a fully charged battery before needing to be recharged.

Laptop batteries come in different types. Learning about these different types before you buy can help you purchase a laptop that will serve you well for years to come.

Types of Battery

Early laptops featured nickel-cadmium (NiCd) batteries, the first rechargeable batteries manufactured for laptops. NiCd batteries were heavy, could not hold much power and could be recharged only a limited number of times. In addition, NiCd batteries could not be left on the charger after they had reached full charge and could not be recharged until they were completely dead. For these reasons, laptop manufacturers have since abandoned NiCd batteries. Newer laptop batteries address these issues in addition to being more efficient. These include nickel-metal hydride (NiMH) batteries and the more recent, lighter, more efficient and more expensive lithium-ion (LiON) batteries.

Battery Life

Laptop batteries offer a certain number of hours of battery life – that is the period during which the battery is capable of operating at or above a given level after it has been fully charged. When fully charged, the average laptop battery offers anywhere from two to four hours of battery life. This number can vary, however, depending on the type of battery your laptop has, how the laptop is being used and what types of hardware components the laptop has. Batteries with higher milliamperes per hour (mAh) have a longer battery life.

What Affects Battery Life?

Various issues affect the life of a battery. One is whether the laptop is being used or is on standby mode. Another is how long the laptop takes to power down or power up. In addition, having a larger monitor with higher resolution or one used at a higher brightness setting can drain a battery faster. And of course, battery life depends on the type of battery you have. Fortunately, laptop PCs have several tools for prolonging battery life, from dimming the screen display to automatically switching to a standby mode when not in use for a prescribed period of time.

Sleep Mode

One way to stretch your battery life is to put your laptop into Sleep mode when you are not using it. Sleep mode turns off the screen, hard drive and internal fan and generally uses less energy. When your laptop comes out of Sleep mode, whatever you were doing when the laptop went into Sleep mode is still open and available for you to return to work. In Hibernate mode, the laptop is completely powered down; when you restart the laptop, whatever you were doing when the laptop went into Hibernate mode re-appears on the Windows 7 desktop.

Gauging Your Charge

Your laptop keeps you informed of your battery charge in a couple of ways. First, the Windows 7 taskbar displays a battery meter that shows you how much charge you have left. You can also set a low-battery alarm to alert you when power is just about to run out. To learn how to set a low-battery alarm, see Chapter 2.

Charging Your Battery

You will need to charge your laptop battery on a regular basis. You do this by plugging your laptop's power cord into an electrical outlet. Getting in the habit of keeping your battery charged is essential. Unless your laptop has an older battery that requires you to wait until the battery is practically drained to recharge it, your motto should be, "Charge often!"

Run on AC Power

If you are using your laptop at your home or office, you can plug its power adapter into an electrical outlet and run on mains electricity all the time. This has the added benefit of recharging your battery and keeping it fully charged. If you lose your adapter, damage it or it simply stops working, you can buy a replacement. Note, though, that you must find an adapter designed to work with your make and model of laptop.

Add a Second Battery

The easiest way to stretch the time you have to work on your laptop with a battery is to double your battery power by carrying a spare. When the first one runs low, simply swap them out, inserting your spare battery to keep using your laptop. Some laptops are designed with quick-swapping in mind, enabling you to simply eject the spent battery and quickly insert the spare, without even shutting down your system. Other laptops require that you power down your computer first. Note that the spare battery must fit your laptop model chassis; be sure to get the right model battery or it will not work.

Battery Life Expectancy

Different types of batteries have different life expectancies. Although lithium-ion batteries have the longest life spans – about 500 charges – even they eventually wear down. As batteries wear down, they are no longer able to hold a charge for as long as when they were new or may fail to fully charge. If you find yourself in need of a new battery, contact your laptop's manufacturer to purchase one. When purchasing a new battery, beware of generic makes. Always buy a manufacturer's, or manufacturer approved, battery. Be aware that new batteries can be quite expensive.

CONTENTS

2

SETTING UP YOUR LAPTOP PC

When you bring home a new laptop, you will want to take some time to explore how its various components, such as the pointing device and keyboard, operate.

In addition, you will want to set up your laptop so that you can use it as efficiently as possible right out of the gate. This might involve connecting a printer, microphone or other hardware device; changing screen settings; selecting a power plan to maximise battery life; and more.

And of course, you need to master the basics of starting your laptop, getting help and shutting it down.

TURN THE LAPTOP ON AND OFF

You should take a moment to get used to how your laptop computer opens and powers on. Although laptop models vary slightly in how the latch on the laptop case operates, most work in a similar fashion.

When you power on your laptop, Windows 7 displays a Welcome screen. If multiple user accounts are set up on your laptop, you are prompted to select the user account you want to use. Depending on that account's settings, you may also be prompted to enter a password.

When you are finished using your laptop, you should shut it down. Shutting down your laptop when you are not using it is important for conserving energy. In addition to shutting down your laptop, you can choose other options, such as Sleep and Hibernate.

Turn the Laptop On

1 Open the laptop.

2 Press the Power button.

In a few moments, the computer boots up and your operating system's Welcome screen appears.

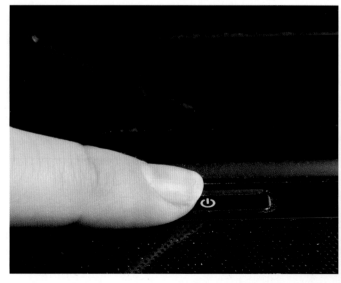

✓ *Close your laptop by pushing the lid down. The slider mechanism automatically engages.*

Turn the Laptop Off

① Click **Start** (📷).

    Ⓐ *To shut down your PC, click* **Shut down**.

② Point to the right arrow (▶) next to the **Shut down** option.

    Windows displays additional choices.

    Ⓑ *Click* **Sleep** *to place your laptop in stand-by mode. It still continues to use some power but nonessential components and operations are suspended.*

    Ⓒ *Click* **Hibernate** *to save your data and power down your computer, keeping your desktop intact. When you restart the system, it reloads the same programs, folders and files.*

    Ⓓ *Click* **Switch user** *to switch to a different user account without closing the programs open in the current account.*

    Ⓔ *Click* **Log off** *to close all open programs and log off from your account. This returns Windows to the Welcome screen.*

    Ⓕ *Click* **Lock** *to lock the computer. Before using the computer, a user must enter any password specified for the current user account.*

    Ⓖ *Click* **Restart** *to close all open programs, shut down Windows and then start it up again.*

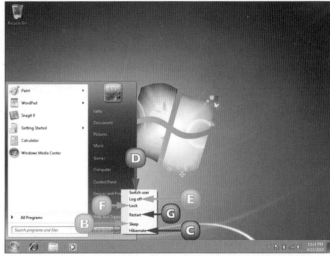

Pressing your laptop's power button or closing its lid puts it in Sleep mode. You can change the behaviour. Right-click the power icon (🔋) in the taskbar and select **Power Options**. *Click* **Choose what the power button does**. *Click* **When I press the power button** ▾ *under* **On Battery** *and choose an option:* **Do Nothing, Sleep, Hibernate** *or* **Shut Down**. *Select an option for* **When I close the lid**. *Click* **Save changes**.

CHARGE THE BATTERY

If you are using your laptop at your home or office, you can power it by plugging it into an electrical outlet. If, however, you are on the road, you can run your laptop on battery power. Most laptop batteries can run for two to four hours, depending on the laptop's setup.

When the battery runs down, you can recharge it by plugging your laptop back into an electrical outlet using the cord that came with it. (The time it takes for a laptop battery to recharge varies; consult your user manual for details.) Keeping your battery charged is essential.

① Plug the power cord into the appropriate slot on your laptop.

② Plug the other end of the power cord into an electrical outlet.

Note: *If you travel internationally, find out what type of electric adapter you need in your destination country. Without such an adapter, you could seriously damage your laptop when you plug it into a wall outlet to charge the battery.*

The power icon in the notification area of the taskbar changes from ▤ to ▣.

CONNECT PERIPHERALS

With Windows 7, connecting a printer, a scanner, a Web cam or other hardware to your laptop is easy. In fact, in most cases, after you connect the device to your laptop via the appropriate port, Windows 7 locates the software it needs to interact with the device (called *drivers*) online and installs it with no input from you.

If Windows 7 is unable to install these drivers, it generally notifies you and offers suggestions on what steps to take next. If Windows 7 fails to do this, you can start a wizard to set up any hardware you connect.

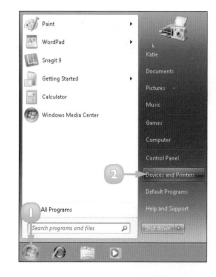

① Click the **Start** button ( ).

② Click **Devices and Printers**.

The Devices and Printers window opens.

③ Click **Add a device** or **Add a printer**.

Windows 7 launches the appropriate wizard.

④ Follow the instructions.

Note: *Simply disconnect the device from your laptop to remove it.*

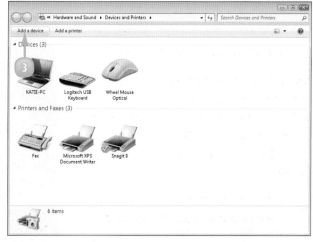

If Windows 7 fails to install the necessary drivers automatically and stepping through the wizard does not resolve the problem, you may need to obtain the necessary drivers from the manufacturer of your device. The easiest way to do this is to visit the manufacturer's website and download the driver. If the device came with a CD or DVD, that disc is likely to contain the necessary drivers to run the device with your laptop.

USE A TOUCHPAD

Your laptop's built-in pointing device can deliver full mouse functionality, enabling you to move the mouse pointer as needed and click to make selections, choose commands and perform other important tasks.

The most common type of laptop pointing device is a touchpad. A touchpad, sometimes called a trackpad, is a flat surface that detects finger contact; you move your finger to move the mouse pointer on screen. Typically there are also two large buttons, usually somewhere beneath the touchpad. You press these buttons to perform traditional left- and right-mouse button functions.

You can also plug a normal USB mouse into your laptop.

1 Place your finger on the touchpad.

Note the position of the mouse pointer on your monitor.

2 Slide your finger around the touchpad.

Note how the mouse pointer moves on the screen.

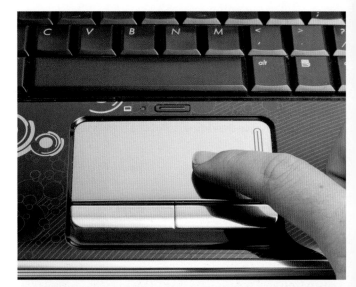

3 Press the left button.

The action that occurs depends on the location of the mouse pointer when you pressed the button. For example, if the mouse pointer was over the Start button when you clicked, the Windows 7 Start menu opens.

4 Press the right button.

A context menu appears.

USE A WIRELESS MOUSE

Many people have difficulty getting used to a touchpad or other pointing device on their laptops. If you find a traditional mouse easier to use, you can purchase a wireless mouse.

A wireless mouse is a natural addition to any laptop. It does not require cables, it is lightweight and it replaces the sometimes awkward touchpad or other pointing device on your laptop with the familiar functionality of the desktop mouse.

Several wireless mice are on the market, including ones made especially for laptops. These are smaller than desktop mice, making them easy to take with you when you travel with your laptop.

The Elements of a Mouse

Mice come in different styles, but most include a right and left button and a scroll wheel. The left button is used for clicking in a file to place your cursor and for clicking and dragging to select objects and text. The right button is used to display shortcut menus. You can roll the scroll wheel to scroll through documents.

How a Wireless Mouse Works

When you purchase a wireless mouse, you also receive a transmitter that plugs into your laptop's USB port. When you plug in the transmitter, Windows 7 typically detects it and installs the necessary software, called a *driver*, for the transmitter and mouse to work. The wireless mouse then overrides the built-in mouse function.

Choose a Mouse

You can find a wireless mouse specifically designed for laptop users. They are smaller than a traditional mouse and easily fit in a small space such as a pocket of a laptop bag. Higher priced versions of wireless mice may feature an extended range and greater precision.

GET TO KNOW THE KEYBOARD

One of the most important features of a laptop is how its keyboard feels to you. Laptop keyboards can vary from those condensed for space – depending on function keys to provide full functionality – to expansive, desktop-style keyboards with number pads and special shortcut keys. Your choice of keyboard is most directly related to the size and weight of laptop that you need.

In addition to the alphanumeric keys that you press to enter text, laptops often include specialised keys. For example, the Windows key (⊞) is used to open the Windows Start menu on a laptop running Windows. Other special keys are discussed here.

Modifying Keys

Several keys on your keyboard are used to modify actions. For example, `Shift`, `Ctrl` and `Alt`, when pressed with another key, modify how that key works. For example, pressing `Ctrl`+`C` copies the selected text or object in a file and pressing `Ctrl`+`V` pastes the copied text or object. And, of course, pressing `Shift` plus any letter capitalises the letter. These combinations of keys are called *keyboard shortcuts*. Note that you can also use many of these keys in conjunction with clicking your mouse or pointing device to perform certain actions. For example, pressing `Ctrl` while clicking files in a folder window enables you to select multiple files.

Navigation Keys

If, like many users, you find it difficult to manoeuvre with the pointing device built into your laptop, you should consider using the various navigation keys to move your cursor around: `End`, `Home`, `Page up`, `Page down`, ↓, ↑, ← and →. Pressing `End` moves the cursor to the end of the current line. Pressing `Home` moves the cursor to the beginning of the current line. Pressing `Page up` or `Page down` moves the cursor up or down one page, respectively. Pressing the directional keys ↓, ↑, ← and → moves the cursor down, up, left and right.

Function Keys

Function keys are available on all laptop keyboards to provide shortcuts to functions in programs. Function keys marked `F1` to `F12` initiate different actions, depending on the program in which you are working. For example, pressing `F1` while working in Microsoft WordPad opens a Windows Help and Support window with links to help articles about WordPad. On a laptop, where space is at a premium, there is often a key labelled `Fn`; by pressing this key along with a function key, you can initiate a different function from the one initiated by pressing the function key alone. For example, on the author's laptop, pressing `Fn` at the same time as `F1` locks the laptop.

Escape Key

Pressing `Esc` stops a current action. In Windows, this key acts as a shortcut for clicking a No button, Quit button, Exit button, Cancel button or Abort button, making it useful if you want to back out of an action or leave a dialog box or other input screen without saving an entry. Pressing `Esc` is also a common shortcut for clicking the Stop button found in many Web browsers, as well as a shortcut for pausing games or displaying a game's menu. This key is typically located in the upper left corner of your keyboard, to the left of the function keys.

Caps Lock Key

Pressing `Caps lock` toggles the Caps Lock feature on and off. With Caps Lock on, anything you type appears in uppercase. With Caps Lock off, everything you type is lowercase and you need to press `Shift` to capitalise a letter, such as the first letter of the first word in a sentence, the first letter in a person's name or the word "I". On many keyboards, a small light becomes illuminated when the Caps Lock feature has been toggled on. Note that toggling the Caps Lock feature does not affect non-letter keys, such as number keys or punctuation keys.

Keys for Cursor Placement

`Enter` is used to start a new paragraph in a text document or to accept an entry in a dialog box. `Spacebar` is used to add a space between letters in a sentence. Press `Del` to delete a selected object or text. Press `Backspace` to move your cursor back one character or space. Press `Insert` to switch from Overtype mode to Insert mode. In Overtype mode, text you type overwrites existing text to the right of the cursor; in Insert mode, existing text to the right of the cursor is moved to the right when you add new text. Press `Tab` to advance the cursor to the next tab stop or to move to the next field in a dialog box.

The Embedded Numeric Keypad

All keyboards feature a row of number keys along the top. The placement of these keys, however, makes entering a lot of numbers difficult. For this reason, most keyboards include a numeric keypad, which is laid out similarly to a calculator, to speed number entry. On most desktop keyboards, this numeric keypad is on the far right. On laptops, where space is limited, the calculator-style numeric keypad is embedded within the letter and number keys on the right of the keyboard. When you turn on the Num Lock feature by pressing `Num lock` or the appropriate function-key combination, those keys turn into numeric-keypad keys.

CONNECT AND TEST A MICROPHONE

If you plan to record sound files, such as narrations for PowerPoint presentations, you need a microphone. You can also use a microphone to take advantage of the Speech Recognition features in Windows 7. Finally, you need a microphone if you intend to use your laptop to communicate with others using VoIP services, such as Skype or MSN.

The first time you connect your microphone to your laptop, you should take a few moments to set it up and make sure that it picks up your voice clearly. To help you with this, Windows 7 includes the Microphone Setup Wizard.

1 After plugging your microphone or headset into the appropriate port on your laptop, click the **Start** button (⊞).

2 In the Start menu's Search field, type **microphone**.

Windows displays a list of items that match what you typed.

3 Click **Set up a microphone**.

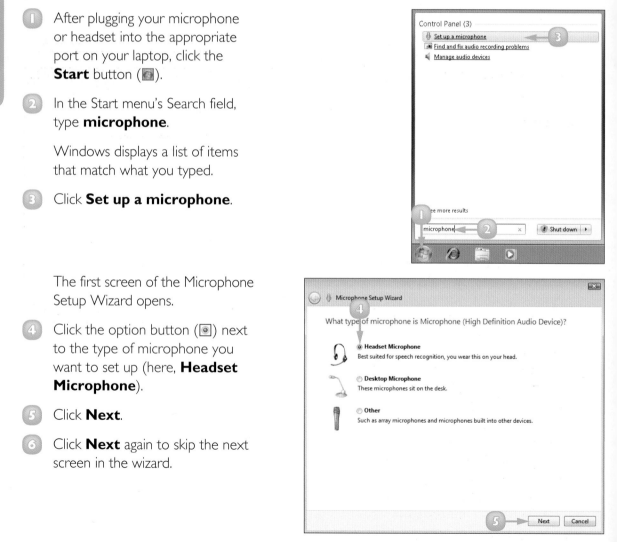

The first screen of the Microphone Setup Wizard opens.

4 Click the option button (◉) next to the type of microphone you want to set up (here, **Headset Microphone**).

5 Click **Next**.

6 Click **Next** again to skip the next screen in the wizard.

30

7 With the microphone situated near your mouth, read the sample sentence.

8 Click **Next**.

Note: *If the wizard informs you that it could not hear your speech, check the connection of your microphone to your laptop and ensure that the microphone's Mute button has not been engaged. Then read the sentence again.*

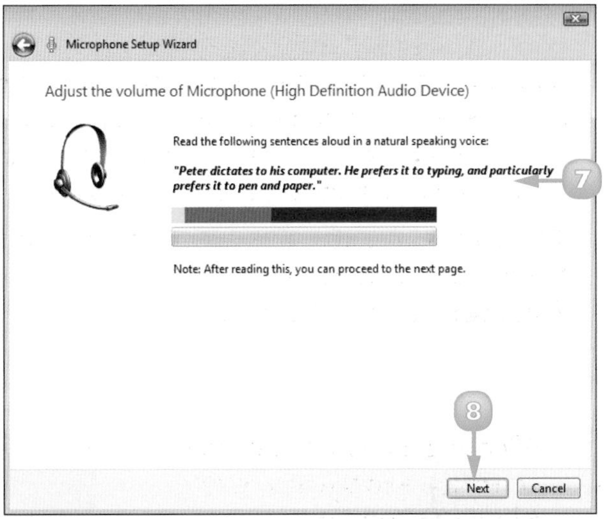

Windows sets up your microphone.

9 Click **Finish**.

✓ *Most laptops have built-in speakers but headphones can be a great way to cut down on sound around you and keep your listening experience private. Headphones come in several types, from clip-on, earbud and ear-canal headphones to earpad-style headphones that fit over your ear to full-size headphones that cover your ears completely. Setting up headphones is a simple matter of plugging them into your laptop's headphone jack. (For help identifying a headphone jack, refer to Chapter 1.)*

Microphone Setup Wizard

Adjust the volume of Microphone (High Definition Audio Device)

Read the following sentences aloud in a natural speaking voice:

"Peter dictates to his computer. He prefers it to typing, and particularly prefers it to pen and paper."

7

Note: After reading this, you can proceed to the next page.

8

Next   Cancel

Microphone Setup Wizard

Your microphone is now set up

The microphone is ready to use with this computer.

Click Finish to complete the wizard.

9 Finish   Cancel

CHANGE THE SCREEN RESOLUTION

You can change your laptop PC's screen resolution. With a higher screen resolution, text and images on your screen appear sharper. In addition, they are smaller, meaning that more items fit on the screen. With a lower screen resolution, items on your screen may appear less crisp, but they are larger and therefore easier to see. Items on a screen with a resolution of 800 × 600 appear much larger than in a screen with a resolution of, say, 1280 × 800.

How you set your screen resolution is largely a matter of personal taste, but larger monitors do often require a higher screen resolution.

① Right-click a blank area of the desktop.

The desktop context menu appears.

② Click **Screen resolution**.

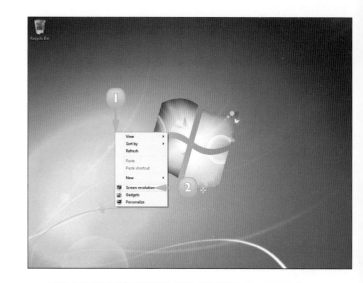

The Screen Resolution window appears.

③ Click the **Resolution** ▼.

④ Drag the **Resolution** slider to the desired resolution.

⑤ Click **OK**.

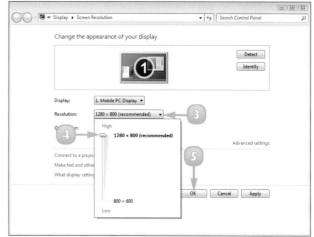

Windows prompts you to confirm the change.

6 Click **Keep changes**.

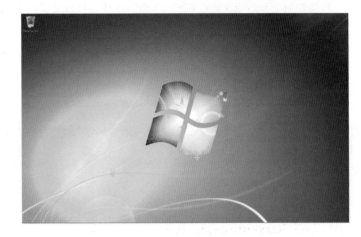

Windows changes the screen resolution.

CHANGE THE DESKTOP BACKGROUND

Your laptop features a default desktop background – most likely one that features a Windows 7 logo or a design supplied by the computer manufacturer.

If you do not like the desktop background that appears by default, you can choose a different image or set of images. One option is to select from the Windows 7 predesigned backgrounds; alternatively, you can choose from favourite photos. A third option is to obtain images online to use for your desktop background.

In addition, you can set a screen saver, which appears after your system has been idle for a prescribed period of time.

① Right-click a blank area of the desktop.

② Click **Personalize**.

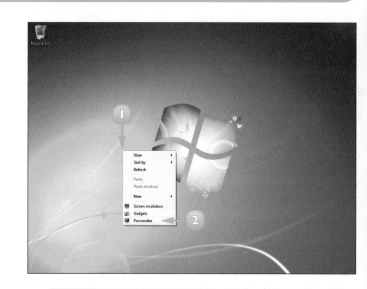

The Personalization window appears.

③ Click **Desktop Background**.

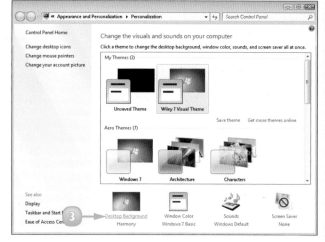

34

The Choose Your Desktop Background window opens.

4 Click the **Picture location** ▼ and select **Windows Desktop Backgrounds**.

   Ⓐ *To choose from your own images, click **Browse,** navigate through the directories to locate your photo folder and then click **OK**.*

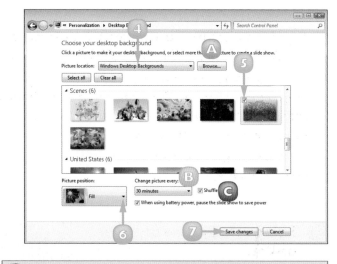

5 Position the mouse pointer over the image you want to use as the desktop background and then click the check box (☑) that appears.

6 Click the **Picture position** ▼ and select the option for how the image should appear on screen.

   Ⓑ *If you have selected multiple images, click the **Change picture every** ▼ and select how often the pictures should change.*

   Ⓒ *To display multiple images in random order, select the **Shuffle** option.*

7 Click **Save changes**.

   Windows changes the desktop background.

8 Click the **Close** button (✖) to close the Personalization window.

✓ *A screen saver is a still or animated picture that appears on your laptop's screen when the pointing device and keyboard have been inactive for* *a prescribed period of time. It prevents others from viewing your desktop when you are away from your laptop. To turn off the screen saver and again view the Windows desktop, simply use your pointing device or press a key on your keyboard. You set a screen saver by choosing it from the Screen Saver Settings dialog box; to open it, right-click a blank area of the desktop, click Personalize and click Screen Saver in the Personalization window.*

VIEW MOBILITY SETTINGS

Windows 7 includes many laptop-specific settings. As you might guess, many of these settings relate to conserving power – something especially critical when you must use a battery to power your PC. For example, you can reduce the brightness of the laptop display to minimise power usage. Others pertain to connecting to the Internet via wireless access points, synchronising your laptop with another PC and giving presentations.

To make it easy to access all these laptop-specific settings, Windows 7 has a special window called Windows Mobility Center. You access this window through the Windows 7 Control Panel.

1 Click **Start** (⊞).

2 Click **Control Panel**.

The Control Panel window appears.

3 Click **Hardware and Sound**.

The Hardware and Sound
window appears.

④ Click **Windows Mobility
Center**.

The Windows Mobility Center
window appears.

Note: *An even faster way to open the
Windows Mobility Center window is to right-
click the power icon ( ) in the taskbar's
notification area and select Windows Mobility
Center from the menu that appears.*

*You can set up your laptop to
conserve power by adjusting
the brightness of the display.
You might also adjust the
display brightness to ease
eyestrain or generally make
your screen easier to see. To
adjust the brightness, drag the
Brightness slider in the
Windows Mobility Center to
the left to make the screen
more dim or drag the slider
to the right to brighten the
screen. For additional
brightness settings, click the
Change Display Brightness
button ( ). The screen that
appears enables you to specify
under what circumstances the
display should be dimmed,
turned off and put to sleep.*

CHOOSE A POWER PLAN

Windows 7 offers three power plans for laptop computers: Power Saver, High Performance and Balanced.

Use Power Saver when the laptop is running on battery. It shuts down various components after the system has been idle for a short period of time to conserve power.

Use High Performance when the laptop is plugged in. It waits longer to shut down components when the system is idle.

Use Balanced, the default, if you do not want to bother changing plans when your power supply changes. It offers a happy medium between Power Saver and High Performance. Note that you can modify plans as needed.

Choose a Different Power Plan

1. In the Windows Mobility Center window, click the **Battery Status** ▾.

2. Click a different plan.

   Windows applies the plan you choose.

Modify a Power Plan

1. In the Windows Mobility Center window, click the **Change Power Settings** button (🔲). The Power Options window appears.

Note: *A faster way to open the Power Options window is to right-click the power icon (🔲) in the taskbar's notification area and select* **Power Options** *from the menu that appears.*

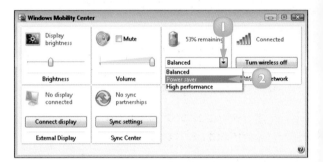

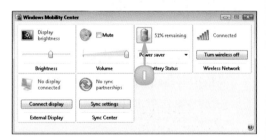

② Click **Change plan settings** for the power plan you want to change.

The Edit Plan Settings page appears.

③ Click the ⏷ to adjust the On Battery options.

④ Click and drag the slider to set the Adjust Plan Brightness setting under the On Battery option.

⑤ Click the ⏷ to adjust the Plugged In options.

⑥ Click and drag the slider to set the Adjust Plan Brightness setting under the Plugged In option.

Ⓐ *For more options, click* **Change advanced power settings**.

⑦ Click **Save changes**.

Set a Low-battery Alarm

① Open the Edit Plan Settings window for your power plan.

② Click **Change advanced power settings**.

③ Click the plus button (⊞) to the left of the **Battery** entry.

④ Click the plus button (⊞) to the left of the **Low battery notification** subentry.

⑤ Click **On battery** to reveal a ⏷, click the ⏷ and click **On**.

⑥ Click **OK**.

⑦ Click **Save changes**.

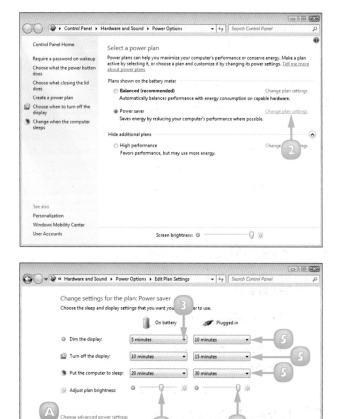

CONTENTS

3

USING SOFTWARE PROGRAMS ON YOUR LAPTOP PC

Laptop PCs running Windows 7 come bundled with several preinstalled programs, also referred to as applications. These preinstalled programs include WordPad, a full-featured word-processing application; Paint, used to create drawings and edit digital images; various games; and a calculator.

In addition to these are countless other programs compatible with Windows 7. Some, like the downloadable programs offered on Microsoft's Windows Live Web site, are free of charge; others are available for purchase.

Although not all programs operate in exactly the same way, many do share common tools and features, as outlined in this chapter.

The Windows 7 desktop serves as the starting point for any task you want to perform using your laptop. For example, from the Windows 7 desktop, you access the Start menu, from which you can launch programs, access files and locate settings for Windows 7.

The Windows 7 desktop also enables you to keep track of what programs you have running, switch among those programs and close them as needed. The desktop also displays important information about your computer's operation.

Familiarising yourself with the various components of the Windows 7 desktop is critical.

A Start Button

Click the **Start** button (⊞) to reveal the Start menu. This menu offers access to available programs, the Windows Help and Support area, the Control Panel and more.

B Desktop Shortcuts

Double-click a shortcut icon to a program or file to launch it. To create a shortcut, right-click the item in the Start menu or Windows Explorer, click **Send To** and then click **Desktop (Create Shortcut)**.

C Taskbar

The taskbar displays icons for all programs you have open. The taskbar features icons for launching Internet Explorer 8, Windows Explorer and Windows Media Player.

D Notification Area

This area displays information about your computer, such as whether it is connected to a wireless network. It also displays alert icons if your system is in need of attention.

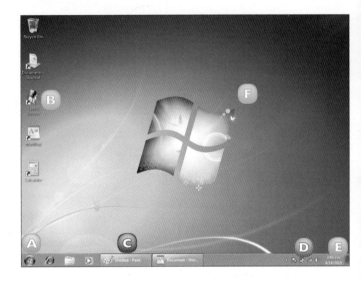

E Show Desktop Button

Click the **Show Desktop** button to minimise any open windows and reveal the desktop.

F Work Area

Windows 7 displays any programs, folders and files that you open in the work area.

Windows 7 comes bundled with several mini-programs, called gadgets. Right-click a blank area of the desktop. Click Gadgets. The Desktop Gadgets window appears. Click the gadget you want to add to your desktop.

START AND EXIT A PROGRAM

Before you can begin working with an application, also called a program, you must instruct Windows 7 to launch it. When you do, Windows 7 starts the program and opens its program window on the desktop.

You can launch an application in few ways. One is to use the Start menu, as described here. Another is to double-click the program's shortcut icon on the desktop (assuming one exists). Some programs – namely, Internet Explorer, Windows Explorer and Windows Media Player – can be launched from the Windows 7 taskbar. Alternatively, you can open a file associated with the program from Windows Explorer.

① Click **Start** (◻).

Ⓐ *If the program you want to start appears in the first pane of the Start menu, click it to launch it.*

② Click **All Programs**. The All Programs menu option changes to a Back menu option.

③ If necessary, click the subfolder containing the program you want to run.

④ Click the program you want to start.

The program you selected opens in a window on the desktop and a button for the program appears in the taskbar.

Note: *A faster way to start a program is to type its name in the Search bar at the bottom of the Start menu. As you type, Windows displays a list of programs that match your text; click the program in the list to start it.*

☑ **You exit a program by closing its window. Click the Close button (◻). The program window and its taskbar button disappear.**

NAVIGATE A PROGRAM WINDOW

When you start a program, its program window appears on the Windows desktop. Although not all program windows are the same, many share certain navigation elements in common. Taking time to familiarise yourself with these elements makes navigating program windows much easier.

These elements include the Window Menu button, the Quick Access toolbar, the title bar, various buttons for resizing and closing the program window, scroll bars, a work area and more. In addition, many programs feature what Microsoft calls the *Ribbon*, which offers an intuitive way to locate and execute commands; other programs have retained traditional pull-down menus and toolbars.

A Title Bar
The program window's title bar displays the name of the program as well as the name the file open in the program window.

B Window Menu Button
Clicking the Window Menu button reveals commands for restoring, moving, sizing, minimising, maximising and closing the program window. (Note that the appearance of this button differs by program.)

C Program Window Controls
Use these buttons to minimise the program window, resize the window or close the window.

D Work Area
The work area is where files you have opened in the program appear. It is where you add and work with data in a program.

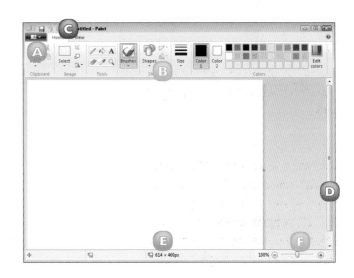

A File Tab

Click the File tab to access options for creating a new file, opening an existing file, saving a file, printing a file and more.

B Ribbon

Some programs feature a Ribbon instead of traditional pull-down menus and toolbars. The Ribbon displays groups of related commands in tabs.

C Quick Access Toolbar

You can use the buttons on this toolbar to launch the Save, Undo or Redo commands. Note that you can change which buttons appear here.

D Scroll Bar

If your file cannot be viewed in its entirety in the work area, drag the vertical and horizontal scroll bars to scroll through the data in the file.

E Status Bar

The status bar displays information about the file currently open in the program window.

F Zoom Controls

Use the Zoom In and Zoom Out buttons or the Zoom slider to zoom your view of the file open in the program window.

RESIZE OR MOVE A PROGRAM WINDOW

Often, you may need to move or resize a program window you have open on your Windows 7 desktop. For example, you might need to make a program window smaller or move a program window in order to view other programs you have running on your laptop or to access an item on your desktop such as a shortcut icon.

In addition to resizing and moving a program window, you can minimise it. When you minimise a program window, you remove it from the desktop; when you are ready to view it again, simply click its button on the taskbar.

Resize a Program Window

① To reduce the size of a window that covers the entire screen, click **Restore Down**.

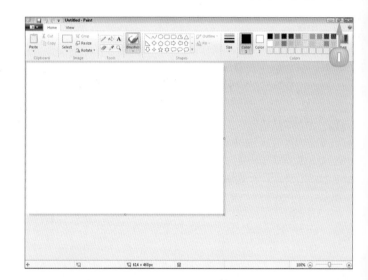

Ⓐ The program window shrinks to a predefined size.

Ⓑ The Restore Down button changes to a Maximize button.

Note: *To maximise the program window so it again covers the entire screen, click the* **Maximize** *button.*

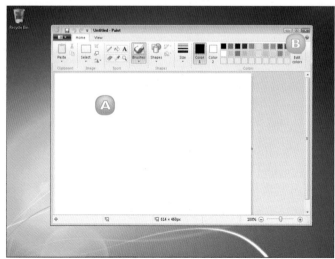

Move a Program Window

① Click an empty section of the program window's title bar.

② Drag the window in the direction you want it to move.

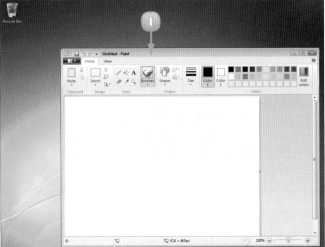

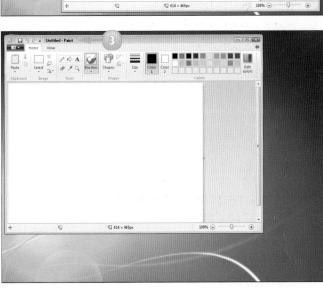

③ When the window is in the desired location, release the mouse button.

 Resizing a window manually enables you to fine-tune its dimensions. Position your mouse pointer over the edge of the window border you want to move. When the pointer changes to a two-headed arrow, click and drag it inward or outward to resize the window and then release the mouse button.

 To minimise a window, click the **Minimize** *button. The program window disappears, but its taskbar button remains in place. To restore the window to its original size and location, simply click its taskbar button.*

47

EXPLORE THE RIBBON

Instead of the menus and toolbars found in many older programs, several Windows 7 applications feature the Ribbon, which offers an intuitive way to locate and execute commands.

The Ribbon is grouped into tabs, each containing groups of related commands. For example, the Home tab in Microsoft WordPad contains commands for changing the font, setting text alignment, indenting text and so on. Some tabs appear only when needed, such as when you are working with a table or picture in a file.

The Ribbon is maximised by default, but you can minimise it to view more of your program window.

Use the Ribbon

1 Click a tab.

The tab organises related tasks and commands into logical groups.

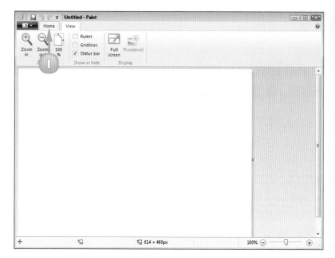

2 Click a button to activate a command or feature.

A Buttons with arrows have additional commands.

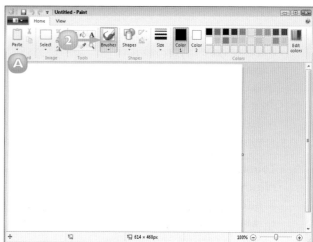

Minimise the Ribbon

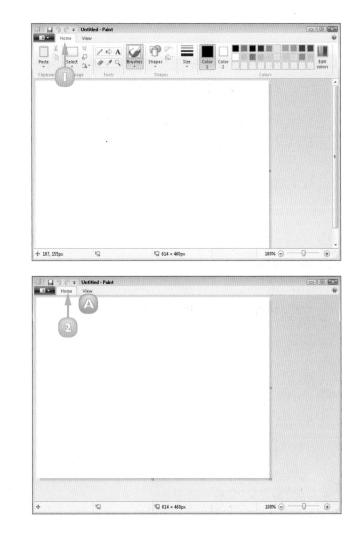

1 Double-click a tab name.

A The Ribbon is minimised.

2 Double-click the tab name again to maximise the Ribbon.

Note: *If you prefer to keep the Ribbon minimised, right-click a tab in the Ribbon and click **Minimize the Ribbon**. To use a Ribbon while it is minimised, simply click the tab containing the tools that you want to access.*

Traditional pull-down menus and toolbars do still exist in certain programs. To use a pull-down menu, click the name of the menu you want to display; then click the command you want to run or the feature you want to enable or disable. (You may need to click a submenu to access the desired command or feature.) To use a toolbar, click the button that represents the command you want to run or the feature you want to enable or disable. (In some cases, clicking an item in a toolbar reveals a drop-down list with additional options; simply click the desired option in the list.)

USE DIALOG BOXES

Often, if a program needs you to supply information, it displays a dialog box. For example, when you save a document for the first time, Windows displays the Save As dialog box; here you can indicate the folder in which you want to save the file, the name you want to give the file and so on.

Dialog boxes feature various types of input controls to enable you to supply information to the program, including drop-down lists, option buttons, spin boxes, check boxes and text boxes.

Many dialog boxes contain a Help button; click it to find out more about the various settings.

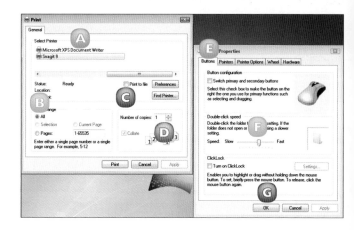

(A) List Box

A list box displays a list of options; you simply click the item you want to select. Scroll bars enable you to move through a longer list to see all available options.

(B) Option Button

You click an option button to enable (⦿) or disable (⦿) the feature associated with it. Only one option button in a group can be enabled at once.

(C) Check Box

Clicking a check box enables (☑) or disables (☑) the feature associated with it. Unlike an option button, multiple check boxes in a group can be enabled at once.

(D) Spin Box

You can click the up and down arrows on a spin box (⬌) to increase or decrease the value in the box, respectively. You can also simply type a value in the text box.

(E) Tab

Some dialog boxes have tabs along the top, each displaying a different set of controls. To switch tabs, simply click the desired tab.

(F) Slider Control

A slider control enables you to made incremental adjustments to a setting.

(G) Command Button

You click a command button to execute the command described on the button – for example, Cancel to close a dialog box without applying your changes.

(A) Text Box

You type text into a text box. For example, you might enter a page range to print in the Print dialog box or the name you want to apply to a file in the Save As dialog box.

(B) Drop-Down List Box

A drop-down list box looks somewhat like a text box, but with a down-arrow button (■) on the side. To change the setting, click the button and select a different option from the list that appears.

✓ **These keyboard shortcuts make dialog boxes easier to navigate.**

Enter	Select the default command button (indicated by a highlight).
Esc	Close the dialog box without implementing your changes (this is the same as clicking the Cancel command button).
Tab	Move forward through the controls in the dialog box.
Shift + Tab	Move backward through the dialog box controls.
↑ or ↓	Move up or down within a group of option buttons.
Alt + ↓	Reveal the available options in the selected drop-down list box.

CREATE OR SAVE A FILE

To work with data in a Windows 7 program on your laptop, you must create a new file in which to store it.

If you want to be able to refer to the data in the file at some later time, you must save the file. You should also frequently save any file you are working on in case of a power failure or computer crash.

When you save a file, you can give it a unique filename, set the file type and store it in any folder you choose. You can then open the saved file at a later time.

Create a File

1 Click the **File** tab.

2 Click **New**.

Note: *Some programs require you to provide additional information when creating a new file. For example, if you are creating a new document in Microsoft Word, you are prompted to indicate what type of document you want to create.*

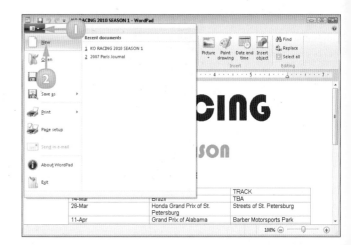

The new file opens.

Note: *An even faster way to create a new file is to press* Ctrl + N.

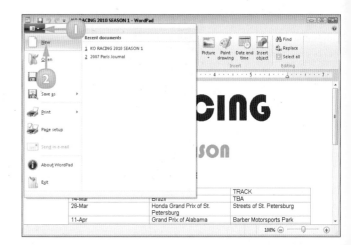

Save a File

① Click the **File** tab.

> **Ⓐ** *For subsequent saves, you can click the **Save** button on the Quick Access toolbar to quickly save the file or press* `Ctrl` + `S`.

② Position your mouse pointer over the **Save as** option.

③ Click a file type.

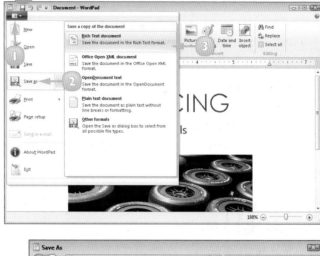

The Save As dialog box appears.

④ In the Navigation pane, click the library in which you want to save the file.

⑤ In the subfolder list, click the folder in which you want to save the file, for example Documents.

⑥ Type a name for the file in the **File name** field.

⑦ Click **Save**.

The program saves the file and the new filename appears on the program window's title bar.

Suppose you are tweaking a form letter that you send out to clients but you want to keep a copy of the original for your records. To do so, launch the Save As dialog box and specify the library and folder in which you want to save the new version of the file, as described in this section. Then type a new name for the file in the File Name text box (so you do not overwrite the original file by accident) and click Save. Windows 7 saves the file in the folder you choose, with the name you indicated.

OPEN A FILE

In addition to creating new files, you can open files that you have created and saved previously in order to continue adding data or to edit existing data.

Regardless of whether you store a file in a folder on your computer's hard drive or on a CD, you can easily access files using the Open dialog box. If you are not sure where you saved a file, you can use the Open dialog box's Search function to locate it.

When you are finished using a file, you should close it. Closing files and programs frees up processing power on your computer.

1 Click the **File** tab.

A *If the file you want to open is listed under Recent Documents, you can click it to open it.*

2 Click **Open**.

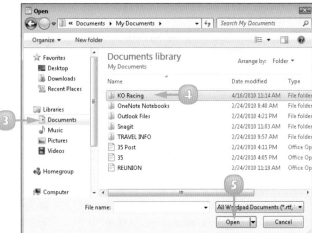

The Open dialog box appears.

Note: *Another way to launch the Open dialog box is to press* Ctrl + O.

3 In the Navigation pane, click the library in which the file you want to open has been saved (here, **Documents**).

4 In the file list, locate and click the folder in which the file you want to open has been saved.

5 Click **Open**.

6 Click the name of the file that you want to open.

7 Click **Open**.

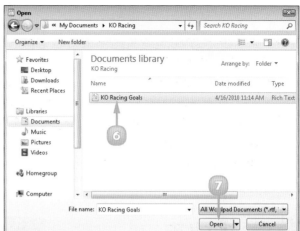

The file opens in the program window.

✓ **To close a file, click the File tab and click Exit in the screen that appears. Alternatively, click the 📧 button in the upper right corner of the program window. Windows 7 closes the file and the program window. As mentioned, closing files frees up processing power on your computer.**

✓ **You can use the Search box in the upper right corner of the Open dialog box to locate files. Simply locate and open the folder in which you believe the file was saved and type the file's name in the Search box.**

PRINT A FILE

If you have connected a printer to your laptop (either via a cable or through a wireless network), you can create printouts of your files. For example, you might distribute printouts of a file as handouts in a meeting.

When you print a file, you can send a file directly to the printer using the default settings or you can open your program's Print dialog box to change these settings. For example, you might opt to print just a portion of the file, or multiple copies of a file, collate the printouts and so on.

① Click the **File** tab.

Ⓐ *The File menu opens.*

② Position your mouse pointer over the **Print** option.

Ⓑ *To print the file using the default settings, click **Quick print**.*

③ Click **Print**.

The Print dialog box appears.

Note: *Another way to open the Print screen is to press* Ctrl + P.

C *You can select a printer from the **Select Printer** list.*

D *You can specify the number of copies to print using the **Number of Copies** spin box.*

E *You can print a selection from the file or specific pages using the available settings in the **Page Range** area.*

④ Click **Print**.

The program sends the file to the printer for printing.

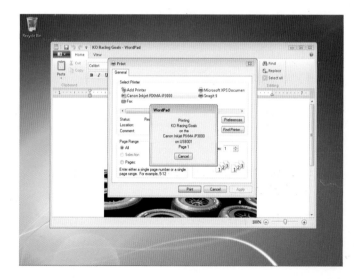

If your printer is designed to connect to your laptop via a USB cable, simply connect it to your laptop; Windows 7 detects the printer and takes the appropriate steps to set it up. If the printer uses another type of cable, connect it to the laptop, launch the Print dialog box and double-click Add Printer in the Select Printer area. Windows 7 launches the Add Printer wizard; click Add a local printer and follow the prompts. If the printer is a network printer, follow these same steps but click Add a network, wireless or Bluetooth printer in the Add Printer wizard.

INSTALL A PROGRAM

Few people limit themselves to using only the programs that came installed on their laptop. Odds are, over time you will want to install additional programs. Windows 7 is designed to make this as easy as possible.

The ins and outs of installing a program differ by program. Some programs are downloaded from the Internet, others from a CD or DVD. The precise steps required are as different as the programs themselves. Do not let this deter you from installing programs on your laptop. Windows 7 is designed to guide you step by step through the installation process.

① Insert the CD or DVD for the program.

② Alternatively, download the program from the Internet and click **Run** when prompted.

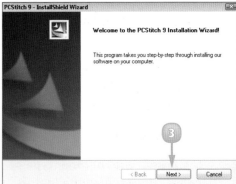

Windows 7 launches the InstallShield Wizard, a tool for installing programs.

③ Click **Next**.

After you select the desired settings in the wizard, it gives you the opportunity to review your choices.

 *To change any of your choices, click **Back**.*

4 If the settings are correct, click **Next**.

The InstallShield Wizard informs you when setup is complete.

5 Click **Finish**.

Uninstall a Program

1 Click the **Start** button (⊙) and select **Control Panel**.

2 In the Control Panel window, click **Uninstall a Program** under Programs.

3 The Programs and Features window opens. Click the program you want to remove.

4 Click **Uninstall**.

5 Windows 7 prompts you to confirm the removal of the program. Click **Yes**. The program is removed.

Note: *If a program has a Change or Repair button in the Programs and Features window, you can change its configuration or repair it in the event it becomes damaged.*

59

CONTENTS

4

NAVIGATING FILES AND FOLDERS IN WINDOWS 7

Windows 7 includes a program called Windows Explorer. It acts like a digital filing cabinet, with folders to store your files and programs.

Windows Explorer enables you to *manage* your files – to copy and move them, rename them as needed and delete them when you are finished using them.

When you open a folder in Windows Explorer, it appears in its own folder window. Folder windows contain several panes to make it easier to find the files you need. They also include a toolbar with various options, as well as a Search field to help you locate the files you need.

VIEW AND OPEN FILES AND FOLDERS

Windows Explorer acts like a digital filing cabinet, with folders to store and organise your files and programs. Each folder contains tools for searching, navigating and organising the files and subfolders within it.

Windows Explorer contains three main folders, called libraries, for storing files. The Documents library is where word-processor files, spreadsheets and Web pages are stored by default. The Pictures library acts as a central repository for digital image files. The Music library is where audio files that you download or rip are saved. In addition, Windows Explorer contains a Videos library.

View and Open Folders

1. Click **Start** (▣).

2. Click **Documents**, **Pictures** or **Music**.

A Windows Explorer folder window opens, displaying the contents of the library you chose.

3. Double-click the folder that contains the file you want to open.

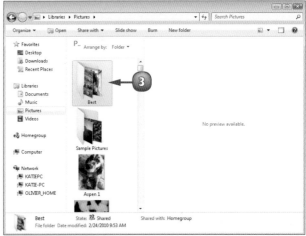

✓ *A faster way to launch Windows Explorer is to click the Windows Explorer taskbar button (▣). The Libraries folder opens, providing quick access to the Documents, Music, Pictures and Videos libraries.*

The folder opens and its contents appear in the File list. The Preview pane shows the selected file.

Open a File

1 Double-click the file you want to open.

Windows opens the file in the default program.

2 Alternatively, to open the file in a different program, right-click the file.

3 Click **Open with**.

4 Click the program you want to use to view or edit the file.

Windows opens the file in the program you choose.

CREATE A NEW FOLDER

Windows Explorer contains several predefined folders (libraries), such as Documents, Pictures, Music and Videos. In addition to these, you can create your own folders. Creating folders makes it much easier to keep your files organised.

For example, you might create a subfolder in your Documents folder for one of your clients to contain any correspondence or other files that pertain to that client. Alternatively, you might create folders for each project you are working on to store all the files associated with each project or you might create a folder to store all your photographs from a recent trip.

1 Open in Windows Explorer the folder in which you want to create the new folder.

2 Click the **New folder** button.

A *Windows creates a new folder with the default name, New Folder, selected.*

3 Type a descriptive name for the new folder and press Enter.

RENAME A FILE OR FOLDER

Giving your files and folders descriptive names makes it easier to keep things organised. If a file or folder's current name is not adequately descriptive, you can rename it. File and folder names can be as long as 255 characters, although the following characters cannot be used:

< > , ? : \ *

You should only rename files and folders that you have created yourself or that have been given to you by others. Never rename Windows system files or folders or files or folders associated with programs installed on your computer. Otherwise, your computer could behave erratically or even crash.

① Click the file or folder you want to rename to select it.

② Right-click the selected file or folder.

③ Click **Rename** from the menu that appears.

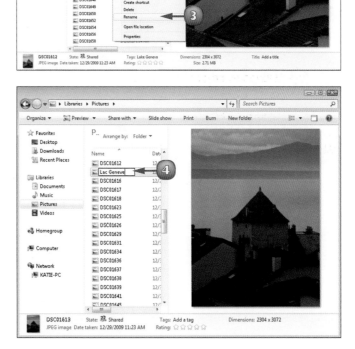

Windows selects the current filename or folder name.

④ Type a new name for the file or folder and press **Enter**.

Windows renames the file or folder.

MOVE AND COPY FILES AND FOLDERS

Most likely, you will populate Windows Explorer with many files and folders over time. If you place a file in the wrong folder by accident or simply create a new folder to store documents you have already created, you must move your files to the correct folder.

In addition to moving files, you can copy them. Copying a file creates two versions of it – one in the original location and one in the new location.

Note that the steps for moving and copying files, covered here, are the same as the steps for moving and copying folders.

Move Files

1 Select the files you want to move.

2 Click the **Organize** button.

3 Click **Cut**.

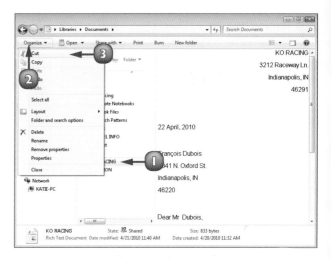

4 Open the folder into which you want to move the selected files.

5 Click the **Organize** button.

6 Click **Paste**.

The selected files are moved from the old location to the new one.

Copy a File

1 Select the files you want to copy.

2 Click the **Organize** button.

3 Click **Copy**.

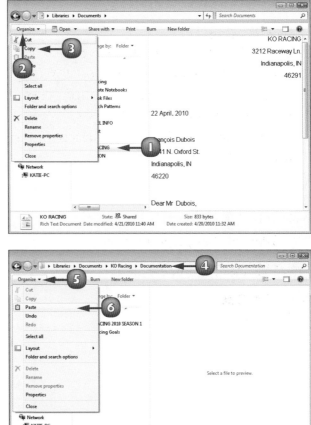

4 Open the folder into which you want to copy the selected files.

5 Click the **Organize** button.

6 Click **Paste**.

Copies of the selected files are placed in the new location.

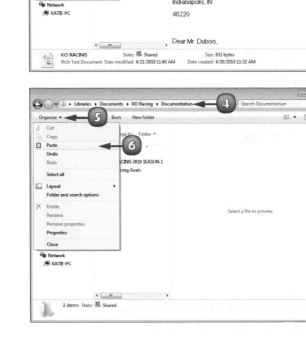

Copy a File to a CD or DVD

1 Select the files you want to copy, or *burn,* to disc.

2 Click the **Burn** button in the folder window toolbar.

3 When prompted, insert a blank disc into the drive.

4 Windows displays the Burn a Disc dialog box; type a title for your disc.

5 Click **Like a USB Flash Drive** to create a data CD or DVD (as opposed to a music CD or video DVD).

6 Click **Next**.

Windows formats the disc and then copies the files.

SEARCH FOR FILES AND FOLDERS

As you work with more and more files and folders on your PC, finding the one you need can become difficult. Fortunately, Windows Explorer offers a robust search function. If you have a general idea where the file or folder you are looking for is located – say, somewhere in your Documents folder – you can use the Search box found in the Documents folder window to search for the file or folder.

You can search using various criteria including name, file type, author, date, even words or phrases that appear within the file (assuming you are searching for a text file as opposed to a digital image or music file).

① Click in the **Search** box.

② Type part or all of the file's name, type, author or other criteria.

    Ⓐ As you type, Windows displays files and folders within the current folder that match your criteria.

SORT, FILTER AND TAG FILES

If you have lots of files in a folder, you can sort them based on various file properties. By default, files are sorted by name, but you can sort by any other property, including Date Modified, Author, Type, and so on.

You can filter files such that only those files with a particular property value are shown in the folder window. For example, you might opt to display those files of the TIFF file type.

You can also apply tags – brief descriptions – to certain types of file and use them as sort, filter, and search criteria. To sort, filter and tag files, the folder window must be in Details view. To switch to Details view, click the Change Your View ▾ and click Details.

Sort Files

1 Click the column header that contains the property by which you want to sort – for example, the Size header.

Note: *To hide the Preview pane, click the* **Hide Preview Pane** *button (▢). Click the same button to reveal the pane.*

Windows Explorer sorts the files by the property you clicked.

Filter Files

1 Position your mouse pointer over the column header for the property you want to filter (here, Type).

2 Click ▾ to see a list of values associated with the column's property.

3 Click the check box with the property value by which you want to filter. Windows displays only the files with the property value you choose.

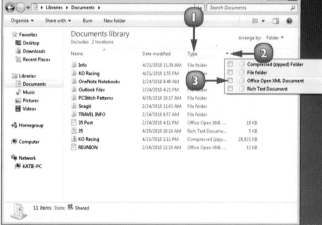

You can tag files. Select a file. Click Add a tag. Type tags separated with semicolons (;). Click Save.

DELETE FILES OR FOLDERS

If you no longer need a file or folder, you can delete it. Deleting unwanted files and folders can help you avoid cluttering your Windows system.

As with renaming files and folders, you should delete only files and folders that you create yourself or that others have given to you; otherwise, your system may begin acting strangely or even crashing.

Deleting a file or folder moves it to the Recycle Bin, where it remains until the Recycle Bin is emptied or until Windows removes the file or folder to make room for other deleted items. As long as neither of these events has occurred, you can restore files and folders you have deleted to their original location.

1 Select the files or folders you want to delete.

2 Click the **Organize** button.

3 Click **Delete**.

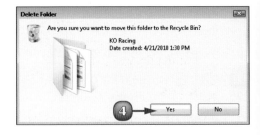

Windows prompts you to confirm the deletion.

4 Click **Yes**.

A The file is deleted from the folder window.

B The Recycle Bin icon on the desktop changes to indicate it is no longer empty.

Empty the Recycle Bin

1 Right-click the Recycle Bin icon on your desktop.

Note: *If you cannot see the desktop because you have program and/or folder windows open, click the* **Show Desktop** *button on the rightmost edge of the taskbar.*

2 Click **Empty Recycle Bin**.

A Windows prompts you to confirm that you want to permanently delete the files in the Recycle Bin.

3 Click **Yes**.

Windows empties the Recycle Bin.

✓ **You can restore items you have deleted. Right-click the Recycle Bin icon on the desktop. Click Open. The Recycle Bin window appears. Select the item you want to restore. Click the Restore This Item button in the window's toolbar. Windows removes the file from the Recycle Bin, placing it back in its original location.**

CONTENTS

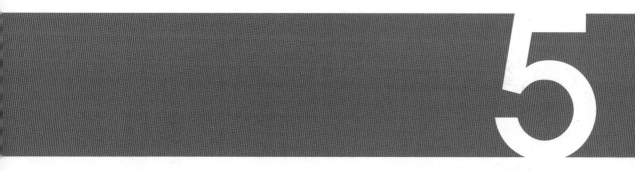

WORKING WITH IMAGES ON YOUR LAPTOP PC

Windows 7 includes several tools for working with digital images, including the Pictures folder, Windows Photo Viewer and Paint. You can also use Windows Live Photo Gallery, a free program available from the Windows Live Web site.

Although the Pictures folder, Windows Photo Viewer and Paint have their uses, Windows Live Photo Gallery has many more features, enabling you to view organise and edit your digital pictures. Windows Live Photo Gallery also makes it easy to share your photos, with tools for e-mailing, printing and posting your photos online as well as for ordering prints.

IMPORT IMAGES TO YOUR LAPTOP PC

To view and edit your digital photos on your laptop, you must first import them from the digital camera you used to capture them.

One way to make the images stored on your camera's memory card accessible to your laptop is to use a cable to connect the camera directly to your computer. Another method is to remove the memory card from the camera, insert it into a memory-card reader and then plug the memory-card reader into your PC's USB port. If your laptop boasts a built-in memory-card reader, you can simply insert the memory card into it.

① Insert your memory card or connect your camera to your laptop.

② In Windows Live Photo Gallery, click **File**.

③ Click **Import from a camera or scanner**.

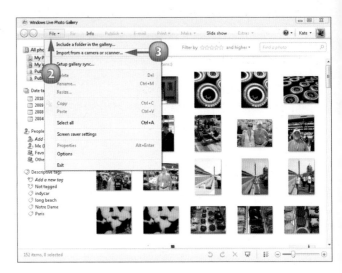

The Import Photos and Videos Wizard starts.

④ Click the icon for your camera or memory card.

⑤ Click **Import**.

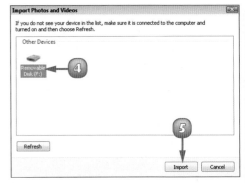

The Import Photos and Videos Wizard detects any image or video files on your camera or memory card.

6 Click the **Review organize and group items to import** option button (◉).

7 Click **Next**.

8 Make sure the check box next to each group you want to import is checked (☑).

9 Click **Import**.

Windows Live Photo Gallery imports the images from your camera or memory card to your laptop.

Many people have albums or shoeboxes stuffed with photos taken with a traditional film-based camera – left over from before they went digital. If you are one of these people, you can use a scanner to convert these photo prints to digital images. Connect your scanner to your PC; Windows 7 should detect it and install the necessary drivers. Then place a photo print in the scanner as outlined in the scanner's manual. Finally, in Windows Live Photo Gallery, click File, click Import from a camera or scanner, click the scanner in the list of devices that appears and click Import.

MANAGE IMAGES IN WINDOWS LIVE PHOTO GALLERY

When you start Windows Live Photo Gallery, you may be prompted to sign in to the Windows Live Web site, which enables you to create online photo albums that you can share with your friends and family. (You will learn how to create and share these albums later in this chapter.)

An important part of organising your photos in Windows Live Photo Gallery is giving them descriptive names. This makes it easier to locate the photos you want to view and edit. To expedite this, Windows Live Photo Gallery enables you to rename image files in batches.

Just as you can apply tags to picture files in the Pictures folder window, you can apply tags using Windows Live Photo Gallery. You can also apply special tags that identify the people in your photos. This makes it easier to sort and locate photos of your friends and family.

Log in to Windows Live

1 Click the **Start** button ().

2 Click **All Programs**.

3 Click **Windows Live**.

4 Click **Windows Live Photo Gallery**.

A *The Sign In to Windows Live dialog box appears.*

B *You can also click* **Sign in** *to open it.*

5 Type your Windows Live ID.

6 Type your Windows Live password.

7 Click **Sign In**.

Batch-Rename Photo Files

1 In Windows Live Photo Gallery, select the pictures you want to batch-rename.

Note: *To select multiple pictures, press* Ctrl *as you click each picture.*

2 Right-click a selected picture.

3 Click **Rename**.

76

The Info pane opens with the contents of the Filename field selected.

 4 Type a name for the files and press **Enter**.

Windows Live Photo Gallery applies the name to each selected picture along with a sequential number to differentiate the files.

Tag Photo Files

1 In the Windows Live Photo Gallery window, select the picture or pictures you want to tag.

2 Click **Info** along the top of the window to display the Info pane.

3 Click **Add descriptive tags**.

4 Type a tag and press **Enter**.

Note: *If adding multiple tags, separate them with commas.*

A *To add a people tag, click* **Add people tags***. Then select from the list of names that appears or type a new name in the blank field. To tag yourself, select* **That's Me!**

VIEW AND OPEN IMAGES IN WINDOWS LIVE PHOTO GALLERY

Windows Live Photo Gallery displays photos as thumbnail-sized images by default. You can view larger versions of your images in Windows Live Photo Gallery in a few different ways. One is to display a preview of the image; another is to open the image in its own screen. If, for example, you need to edit an image, you must open it in its own screen.

After you open an image, you can return to the main Windows Live Photo Gallery window by clicking the Back to Gallery button in the upper left corner of the window.

You can also view a group of images one after another as a slide show.

Open an Image in a Window

1. Position your mouse pointer over the image you want to preview.

   A. *Windows Live Photo Gallery displays a preview of the image.*

2. Double-click the image.

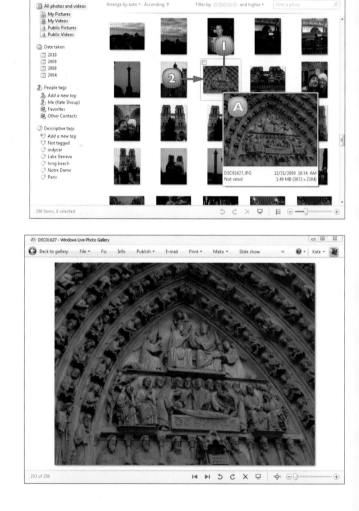

The image opens in its own window.

78

View Images as a Slide Show

1. In Windows Live Photo Gallery, select the pictures you want to view.

Note: *To select multiple pictures, press* Ctrl *as you click each picture.*

2. Click the **Slide show** button.

   A. *You can also click Slide show or press* F12 *or* Alt+S.

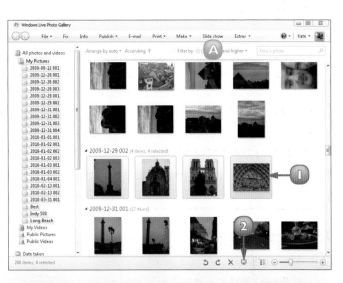

Windows Live Photo Gallery uses the full screen to display the images one at a time.

EDIT A PHOTO

If an image lacks in contrast, seems slightly off in colour or is a bit skewed, you can use Windows Live Photo Gallery's Auto Adjust tool to fix these problems automatically. The Auto Adjust tool automatically applies the Adjust Exposure, Adjust Color and Straighten Photo fixes. (You can, if you prefer, apply these fixes manually on an individual basis.)

If you discover that your image contains some unwanted elements, you can crop those elements out. A photo taken with a flash often shows a person who appears to have red eyes. You can remove this effect.

Before you edit an image, you should make a copy of it and preserve the original. That way, if you are unhappy with the edits, the photo is not permanently damaged.

Auto-Adjust a Photo

1. Open the image you want to auto-adjust.

2. Click **Fix**.

   A. *The Fix pane opens.*

3. Click **Auto adjust**.

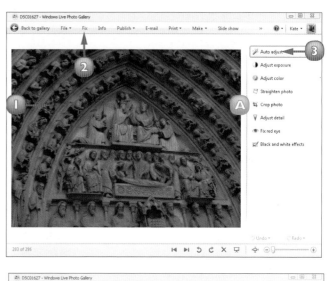

B. *Windows Live Photo Gallery assesses your image, applies the necessary exposure and color settings and straightens the image as needed.*

C. *If clicking Auto Adjust does not yield the desired results, use the Brightness, Contrast, Shadows and Highlights sliders to adjust these settings manually.*

D. *To access the Color Temperature, Tint and Saturation sliders, click **Adjust color**.*

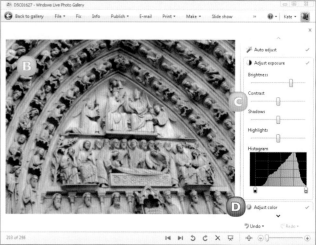

Crop a Photo

1 Open the image you want to crop, click **Fix** and click **Crop photo**.

    A *A cropping frame appears in the image.*

    B *Click the **Proportion** ▾ and select a preset proportion.*

    C *To rotate the crop frame, click **Rotate frame**.*

2 Click and drag the crop frame to the desired spot on the photograph.

    D *To resize the crop frame, click and drag the sizing handles.*

3 Click **Apply**.

Windows Live Photo Gallery crops the photo.

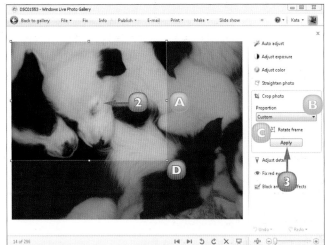

Remove Red Eye

1 Open the image you want to correct.

2 Click **Fix**.

3 In the Fix pane, click **Fix red eye**.

4 Click the upper left corner of an eye that needs correcting.

5 Drag the cursor to the lower right corner of the eye to select the eye.

    A *Windows Live Photo Gallery removes the red eye.*

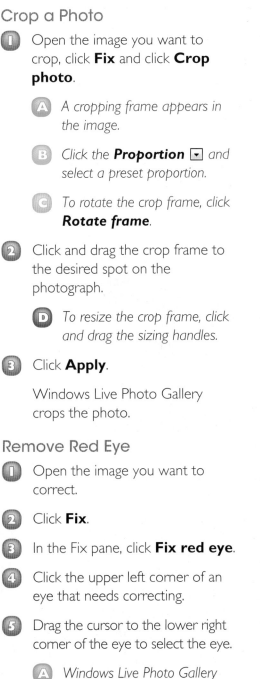

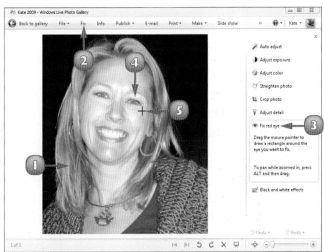

CREATE AND PUBLISH AN ONLINE PHOTO ALBUM

A great way to share your digital photos with others is to publish them in an online album on Windows Live. After you publish the album, you can e-mail a link to that album to others, who can then view and even comment on your photos. As an added benefit, publishing your photos online protects you by giving you access to copies of all your precious photos in the event your hard drive were to fail.

Note that you must be signed in to Windows Live to publish an album. If you are not signed in, click the Sign In button in the upper right corner of the Windows Live Photo Gallery window and follow the on-screen instructions.

1 In the Windows Live Photo Gallery window, select the pictures you want to include in the album.

2 Click **Publish**.

3 Click **Online album**.

The Publish Photos on Windows Live dialog box opens.

A To add the photos to an album you have already created, click it.

4 To create a new album, type a name for the album.

5 Click the album's ⏷ and select who should be permitted to view the album.

6 Click **Publish**.

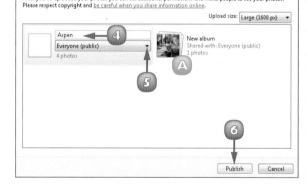

Windows Live Photo Gallery
uploads the selected images to
the Windows Live Web site and
notifies you when the upload
operation is complete.

⑦ Click **View album** to view the
album online.

Windows Live opens in your
Web browser, with the page
containing your album on display.

Note: *To e-mail a link to your album to
others, click* **Share** *and click* **Send a Link.**
*The Send a Link screen opens; type your
recipients in the To field, type a message and
click* **Send.**

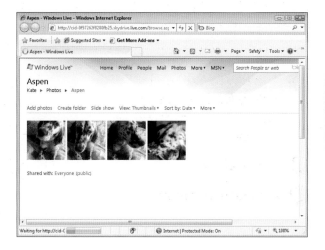

✓ **You can access an online album
by directing your Web browser
to the Windows Live Web site
(home.live.com). Sign in to your
account, click the Photos link,
click All Albums and click the
album you want to view.**

✓ **To print a photo using your own
printer, open the image you
want to print in Windows Live
Photo Gallery, click Print and
click Print. The Print Pictures
dialog box opens; click Print. To
order prints online, select the
pictures you want to order, click
Print and click Order Prints.
The Order Prints Wizard starts;
click a printing provider, click
Send Pictures and follow the
on-screen instructions.**

CONTENTS

6

ENJOYING AUDIO AND VIDEO WITH WINDOWS MEDIA PLAYER

Using the Windows Media Player software that comes bundled with Windows 7, you can organise your media collection, play back your audio and video files, listen to CDs, watch DVDs, rip music from CDs in your personal library, create playlists of your favourite songs, create mix CDs, sync your audio and video files to a portable media player and more.

Assuming your laptop is connected to the Internet, you can also use Windows Media Player to shop for music online, listen to Internet radio broadcasts and access video content such as movie previews.

BUILD YOUR MEDIA LIBRARY

Audio and video files in your Windows 7 Music and Video folders appear in the Windows Media Player library by default. To further build your media library, you can use Windows Media Player to *rip* (copy) tracks from CDs in your collection (assuming your laptop has a CD drive) or to obtain content online.

Of course, although Windows Media Player makes it easy to rip, burn, store and organise your digital media, it is up to you to avoid copying, or otherwise using, copyrighted material without authorisation. Unauthorised use of such materials may subject you to criminal or civil penalties.

Rip Tracks from a CD

1 With Windows Media Player open, insert the CD that contains the tracks you want to rip in your computer's CD drive.

A *Windows Media Player displays a list of the tracks on the CD.*

B *By default, all tracks on the CD are selected. To deselect a track, click its check box (□).*

2 Click **Rip CD**.

C *Windows Media Player rips, or copies, the selected tracks to your music library.*

96

Access Online Content

 In Windows Media Player, click the **Media Guide** ⊡.

 Click **Browse all online stores**.

Windows Media Player displays a list of stores.

Note: *The stores available to you may vary depending on your location.*

③ Click a store to enter it.

Note: *Some stores offer content to which you can subscribe; with others, you purchase the content outright.*

 Before you can purchase or subscribe to content from a Windows Media Player online store, you must first create an account with the store. The ins and outs of creating a store account differ by store. For instructions, click the Help link on a store's page.

You can use Windows Live Photo Gallery to import video content from a digital video camera. Follow the steps in Chapter 5. After you import your video, it appears in Windows Media Player by default.

SORT FILES IN WINDOWS MEDIA PLAYER

Over time, your media collection may grow to the point that finding the files you want to listen to or watch may become difficult. To make it easier to find files, Windows Media Player enables you to sort them by title, album, album artist, genre, release date, date taken, filename or rating.

① Click a folder in the folder list.

② Click **Organize**.

③ Click **Sort by**.

④ Select the parameter by which you want to sort – here, Title.

Ⓐ *Windows Media Player sorts the files in the File list.*

Note: *An even faster way to sort music files is to click the ▷ to the left of the Music folder in the folder list; then click **Artist**, **Album** or **Genre**. Windows Media Player sorts your files in the File list accordingly.*

SEARCH FOR FILES IN WINDOWS MEDIA PLAYER

You can use Windows Media Player's Search field to search for a media file. For example, you might type the name of the song you seek; Windows Media Player then displays a list of files that match your criteria.

1 Type a keyword or phrase in the Search field.

A *Windows Media Player displays a list of files that match your criteria in the File list.*

To rate a file in Windows Media Player, simply locate it in the File list and click the star in the Rating column that represents the rating you want to apply. For example, to give the file a two-star rating, click the second star. If no rating column is shown, right-click the file you want to rate, click **Rate** in the menu that appears and then click the appropriate star.

You can use Windows Media Player to listen to music on your laptop in a few different ways. One approach is to play back audio files stored on your laptop's hard drive. Assuming you have located the song or album you want to hear in Windows Media Player, playing it is as simple as clicking a button.

1 Click the **Music** folder.

2 Double-click the song or album you want to hear.

Windows Media Player plays back the song or album.

A The **Play** button (▶) changes to a **Pause** button (⏸).

B Drag the **Volume** slider to adjust the volume.

C To mute the volume, click the **Mute** button (🔊). It changes to a **Sound** button (🔇); click it to unmute the volume.

D To shuffle the order in which songs are played back, click the **Shuffle** button (🔀).

E To play back a song or play list more than once, click the **Repeat** button (🔁).

F To stop playback, click the **Stop** button (⏹).

G To return to the previous song, click the **Back** button (⏮).

H To skip to the next song click the **Next** button (⏭).

PLAY A CD

If your laptop has a CD drive, you can insert a CD and use Windows Media Player to listen to tracks on that CD. You can also use Windows Media Player's Media Guide feature to access Internet radio stations.

1 With Windows Media Player open, insert the CD that contains the tracks you want to hear into your computer's CD drive.

A *Windows Media Player displays a list of the tracks on the CD.*

B *By default, all tracks on the CD are selected. To deselect a track, click its check box (☐).*

Windows Media Player automatically plays back the selected songs on the CD.

Note: *You use the same controls when playing a music CD as you do when playing back music files on your hard drive.*

Listen to Internet Radio

1 Click the **Media Guide** button in the bottom left corner of the Windows Media Player window. (If this button is not visible, click the 🔽 next to the **Online Stores** button and select **Media Guide** from the menu that appears.)

2 Click the **Internet Radio** link.

3 Click a genre. (If the genre you seek is not shown, click the **Show All Genres** link.)

4 The Media Guide displays a list of stations in the genre you chose. Click a station's **Listen** link to listen.

WATCH VIDEOS IN YOUR MEDIA LIBRARY

In Windows Media Player, you can watch video files stored on your computer's hard drive.

When you play a video, Windows Media Player automatically switches to Now Playing mode; to view the player controls, simply position your mouse pointer over the Now Playing window.

1 Click the **Videos** folder.

2 Double-click the video you want to watch.

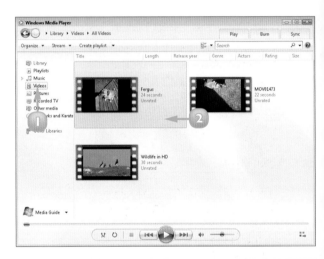

Windows Media Player plays back the video in Now Playing mode.

Note: *You use the same controls when playing a video file as you do when playing back music files.*

PLAY A DVD

You can watch videos by playing a DVD you have inserted into your computer's DVD drive. You can also use Windows Media Player's Media Guide feature to access video content online.

1. With Windows Media Player open, insert into your computer's DVD drive the DVD you want to watch.

2. If the DVD menu does not appear automatically, right-click the DVD in the folder list.

3. Click **Play**.

   Windows Media Player displays the DVD menu in Now Playing mode.

4. Select the desired option from the DVD menu.

   A. *To view the DVD in full-screen mode, click the **View Full Screen** button (■).*

Access Online Video Content

1. Click the **Media Guide** button in the bottom left corner of the Windows Media Player window.

2. Click a link on the main page to view its associated content. Alternatively, click the **Movies** or **TV** link.

3. Select an option from the menu that appears.

4. Click a link in the page that appears to view its associated content.

CREATE AND SAVE PLAYLISTS

If you want to listen to more than just a single song or a single album or to watch multiple videos in a row, you can stack up files in a playlist. Windows Media Player then plays the songs or videos in your playlist in the order you specify.

If you develop a playlist you particularly like, you can save it. When you save a playlist, you can then open it in a later session to listen to the set of songs or view the videos it contains. You can also burn saved playlists to CD or DVD.

1 Click the **Play** tab to display it.

A *If the Play tab already contains other items, click **Clear list** to remove them.*

2 Click an audio or video file you want to include in your playlist.

3 Drag the selected file to the Play tab.

B *Windows Media Player adds the item to the playlist and begins playing it back.*

④ Add more files to the playlist.

Ⓒ *To sort the playlist, click the* **List Options** *button (☑️), click* **Sort List By** *and select a sort parameter (for example, Title).*

Note: *To move a file in the playlist, click it and drag it to the desired location in the list. To remove a file from the playlist, right-click it and select* **Remove from List** *from the menu that appears.*

⑤ Click **Save list**.

⑥ Type a name for the playlist and press `Enter`.

✓ **To play a saved playlist, click the Playlists entry in the folder pane, click the playlist you want to play and click the Play button. When you play back files in a playlist, you use the same controls as when you play back a video, song or album.**

✓ **To delete a playlist, click the Playlists entry in the folder pane, right-click the playlist you want to delete and select Delete from the menu that appears. Specify whether the playlist should be deleted from your library only or from your library and your computer; then click OK.**

BURN CDS AND DVDS

If your laptop has a CD/DVD drive capable of recording to disc, you can use Windows Media Player to create an audio CD that can be played back on any standard CD player.

In addition, you can burn music as data files to a disc; this enables you to fit many more songs on a single disc. You can also burn video files in this way. When you burn audio or video files to disc as data files, they can be played back only on a computer or other device that supports the data format used.

① Click the **Playlists** folder.

② Right-click the playlist you want to burn to a disc.

③ Click **Add to**.

④ Select **Burn list**.

Note: *Another way to specify the files to burn is to click the* **Burn** *tab to open it and then simply drag items from your Windows Media Player library into it.*

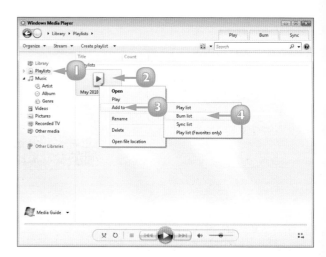

Windows Media Player opens the Burn tab, with the contents of the playlist shown.

⑤ Click **Start burn**.

Windows Media Player prompts you to insert a blank disc.

⑥ Insert a blank recordable disc into your laptop's CD or DVD drive.

Windows Media Player burns the contents of the Burn tab onto the blank disc. (Note that this may take several minutes.)

Ⓐ *Windows Media Player tracks the progress of the burn operation.*

Note: *If the contents of the Burn tab will not fit on a single disc, Windows Media Player gives you the option of burning the remaining items onto a second blank disc.*

🛑 **You cannot use Windows Media Player to create DVDs for playback on a standard DVD player. You can, however, use Windows DVD Maker, also included with Windows 7. See that program's help information for details.**

✓ **To burn song or video files to disc as data files, repeat Steps 1 to 4 in this section. Then click the Burn options button in the Burn tab and select Data CD or DVD from the menu that appears. Next, click Start burn and insert a blank disc when prompted; Windows Media Player burns the files to disc.**

SYNC A MOBILE DEVICE WITH WINDOWS MEDIA PLAYER

Some portable media players and mobile phones can be synced with Windows Media Player. To find out whether your device is compatible, simply connect it to your laptop using the cable provided while Windows Media Player is running.

If the device is compatible, has a storage capacity of more than 4GB and has room to store your entire Windows Media Player library, it syncs automatically (although you can opt to sync only certain playlists if you prefer). All you need to do is click the **Finish** button that appears when the automatic sync is complete. Otherwise, you must sync manually, as covered here.

① Right-click the playlist, song, album, video or other media file that you want to sync to a mobile device.

② Click **Add to**.

③ Select **Sync list**.

Note: *Another way to specify what files to sync is to click the **Sync** tab to open it and then simply drag items from your Windows Media Player library into it.*

Ⓐ *Windows Media Player opens the Sync tab, with the item you specified shown.*

Note: *You can add more files to the Sync tab as needed.*

④ Connect your mobile device to your laptop using the cable provided.

⑤ If necessary, turn the device on.

⑥ Click **Start sync**.

Windows Media Player syncs the
contents of the Sync tab to the
mobile device. (Note that this
may take several minutes.)

B *Windows Media Player tracks
the progress of the sync
operation.*

C *Windows Media Player notifies
you when the sync is complete.*

D *Click* **Click here** *to view the
files that were synced.*

**You can omit a playlist from
an automatic sync. With your
mobile device powered on and
connected to your laptop, click
the Sync tab, click the Sync
options button and select Set
Up Sync from the menu that
appears. Then, in the Windows
Media Player Device Setup
dialog box, click the playlist
you want to omit in the
Playlists to Sync list, click
Remove and click Finish.**

**Windows Media Player cannot
sync with the Microsoft Zune
player. Nor can it sync with
Apple's iPod or iPhone.**

**Several Sony devices are
compatible with Windows
Media Player, as are devices
by Samsung and SanDisk and
various types of Windows
Mobile devices.**

CONTENTS

WORD PROCESSING IN WINDOWS 7

Windows 7 includes a simple word-processing tool called WordPad. WordPad functions like a light version of a commercial word-processing program.

You can use WordPad to handle all your basic word-processing needs, such as viewing documents, writing letters, addressing envelopes, keeping a journal, making lists and so on. You can dress up your WordPad documents by applying different fonts and colours and adjusting spacing, indents and other page properties.

WordPad works with several types of document file format. WordPad saves files in RTF (Rich Text Format) by default.

ENTER AND EDIT TEXT IN WORDPAD

When you launch WordPad or create a new WordPad file, a blank document appears in the WordPad window. (For help creating new files, see Chapter 3.) In the top left corner of that blank document is a blinking cursor, or insertion point, waiting for you to start typing.

Of course, the beauty of any word-processing program is that it enables you to easily edit your text after you type it and WordPad is no exception. With WordPad, you can add new text or delete existing text with the greatest of ease.

Type Text

① Start typing your text.

Ⓐ *WordPad automatically wraps the text to the next line for you.*

Ⓑ *The cursor marks the current location where text will appear when you start typing again.*

② Press **Enter** to start a new paragraph.

Ⓒ *You can press **Enter** twice to add an extra space between paragraphs.*

Ⓓ *You can press **Tab** to quickly create an indent for a line of text.*

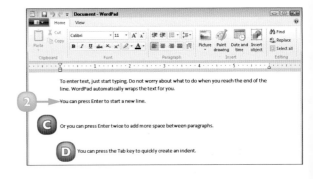

Edit Text

① Click in the document where you want to fix a mistake and start typing.

② Press Backspace to delete characters to the left of the cursor.

③ Press Delete to delete characters to the right of the cursor.

You can also delete selected text.

A blog is a type of Web site that enables an individual or group to share feelings, insights and opinions without having to learn how to use HTML or a Web editor such as FrontPage. You can create and maintain your own blog – for example, to keep in touch with friends and family or to further your career – using Windows Live Writer, an easy-to-use blogging tool from Microsoft that acts like a word processor. You can download Windows Live Writer free of charge from Microsoft's Windows Live Web site.

SELECT TEXT

Before you can perform operations on text – such as deleting it, changing its font or alignment, formatting it as a list, copying and pasting it elsewhere in a document or in a different document altogether and so on – you must select the text. Selected text appears highlighted.

You can select text in a few different ways, using your mouse or your keyboard to select a single character, a word, a sentence, a paragraph or all the text in the document. In this section, you learn how to drag your mouse to select text.

① Click to one side of the word or character that you want to select.

② Drag the cursor across the text that you want to select.

WordPad selects any characters that you drag across.

Ⓐ *To deselect selected text, simply click anywhere outside the text.*

MOVE AND COPY TEXT

You can use the cut, copy and paste commands to move or copy text in WordPad. For example, you might cut or copy a paragraph from a WordPad document and paste it elsewhere in the same WordPad document or in another WordPad document.

When you cut text, it is removed from its original location; when you copy text, WordPad makes a duplicate of the selected data, leaving it in its original location.

1. Select the text you want to move or copy.

2. To move the text, click **Cut**. WordPad removes the selected text from the document.

   A *To copy, rather than cut, the text, click **Copy**. WordPad copies the selected text, leaving it in its original location.*

3. Click the spot in the document (or in another WordPad window) where you want to paste the cut or copied text.

4. Click **Paste**.

   B *The text you cut or copied is pasted in at the specified location.*

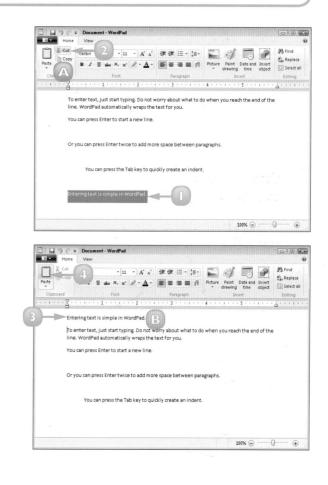

CHANGE THE APPEARANCE OF TEXT

You can change the font, size and colour to alter the appearance of text in a document. For example, if you are creating an invitation, you might make the description of the event a different font and colour to stand out from the other details. Likewise, if you are creating a report for work, you might make the title of the report larger than the information contained in the report or even colour-code certain data in the report.

In addition, you can use WordPad's basic formatting commands – Bold, Italic, Underline, Strikethrough, Subscript and Superscript – to quickly add formatting to your text.

Change the Font

① Select the text you want to format.

② Click the **Home** tab.

③ Click the **Font** ⏷.

④ Click a font.

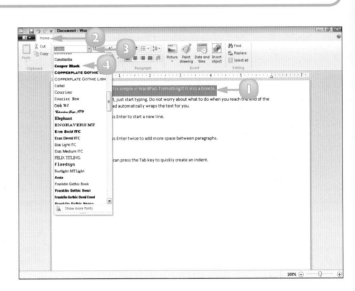

Ⓐ *WordPad applies the font to the text.*

Change the Size

① Select the text you want to format.

② Click the **Home** tab on the Ribbon.

③ Click the **Font Size** ⏷.

④ Click a size.

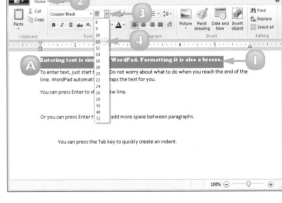

B *WordPad applies the font size to the text.*

C *You can also change the font size by clicking the **Grow Font** button (A) or the **Shrink Font** button (A).*

Change the Colour

1 Select the text you want to format.

2 Click the **Home** tab on the Ribbon.

3 Click the ▾ next to the **Font Color** button (A).

4 Click a colour.

D *WordPad applies the colour to the text.*

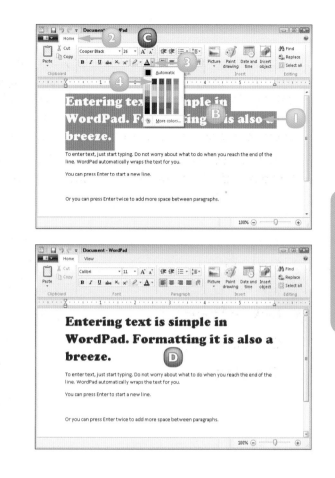

✓ *How do you apply formatting to your text?*

✓ *To apply other formatting to your text, select the text you want to format, click the Home tab and then click the Bold (B), Italic (I), Underline (U), Strikethrough (abc), Subscript (X₂) or Superscript (X²) buttons. WordPad applies the format you choose to the selected text.*

✓ *To format text as a numbered or bulleted list, select the text you want to change, then click the ▾ next to the Start a List button (☰) and select a bulleted or numbered list option from the list that appears. WordPad formats the selected text as a list.*

ADJUST THE POSITION OF TEXT

You can use WordPad's alignment commands to change how text is positioned horizontally on a page, left-aligning text (the default), centring it, right-aligning it or justifying it.

Indents are another way of controlling the positioning of text in a document. For example, you might indent a paragraph, such as a long quote, to set it apart from the rest of the text on the page.

Finally, you can adjust the amount of spacing that appears between lines of text in your paragraphs. For example, you might set double-spacing to allow for handwritten edits in your printed document.

Align Text

1. Select the text you want to align.

2. Click the **Home** tab.

3. Click an alignment button.

   A *Click* **Align Left** *(▤) to left-align text.*

   B *Click* **Center** *(▤) to center text.*

   C *Click* **Align Right** *(▤) to right-align text.*

   D *Click* **Justify** *(▤) to fit text to the left and right margins.*

   WordPad aligns the text.

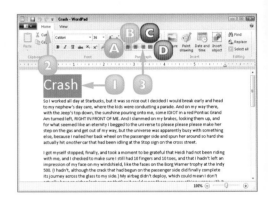

Indent Text

1. Select the paragraphs you want to indent.

2. Click the **Home** tab.

3. Click an indent button.

   A *Click* **Decrease Indent** *(▤) to decrease the indentation.*

   B *Click* **Increase Indent** *(▤) to increase the indentation.*

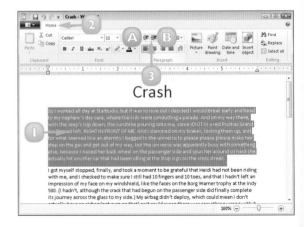

WordPad indents the text.

Set Line Spacing

① Select the paragraphs whose spacing you want to change.

② Click the **Home** tab.

③ Click the **Line Spacing** button (▣).

④ Click a line-spacing option.

Ⓐ *WordPad applies the new spacing.*

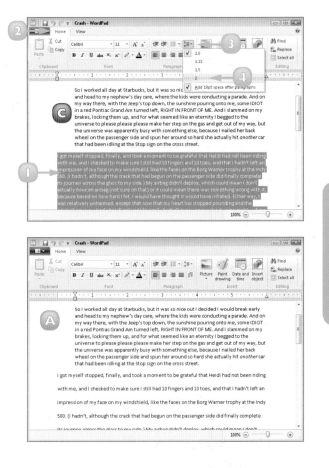

> ✓ **You can set a custom indent using the WordPad ruler. Drag the indent marker (▣) on the ruler to the desired location. If the ruler is not shown in the WordPad window, click the View tab and select the Ruler check box (☑).**

> ✓ **If you realise you have made a change to your document in error, you can undo it. Simply click the Undo button (▣) in the Windows 7 Quick Access toolbar. If, after undoing a change, you realise you want to redo it, click the Redo button (▣), also in the Quick Access toolbar.**

FIND AND REPLACE TEXT

Suppose you are writing a story and you decide to change the main character's name. Or perhaps you realise after writing a report for work that you have consistently misspelled the name of the product you analysed. Either way, you can use WordPad's Replace tool to rectify the situation.

If you simply need to find text rather than replace it, you can use the Find tool. For example, if you need to review a section of your document that is several pages down, you can use the Find tool to search for the title of that section instead of scrolling down to locate the section.

① Click the **Home** tab.

② Click **Replace**.

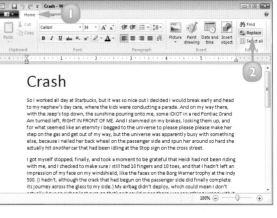

The Replace dialog box opens.

③ In the **Find what** field, type the word or phrase you want to find.

④ In the **Replace with** field, type the replacement text.

Ⓐ *Select the **Match whole word only** check box (☑) to find instances of the text only as a complete word.*

Ⓑ *Select the **Match case** check box (☑) to find instances of the word with the same capitalisation.*

⑤ Click **Find Next**.

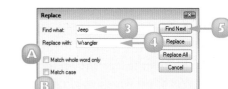

WordPad locates and highlights the first instance of the word or phrase you typed in the Find What field.

6 Click **Replace** to replace only the highlighted text with the word or phrase in the Replace With field.

 *Click **Replace All** to replace all instances of the highlighted text with the Replace With text.*

E *WordPad replaces the selected text with the Replace With text.*

F *WordPad highlights the next instance of the text in the Find What field.*

7 Repeat Step **6** until all instances of the text in the Find What field have been reviewed or replaced.

Note: *WordPad notifies you when it has finished searching the document for the text in the Find What field; click **OK**.*

If you simply need to find text rather than replace it, click the **Find** button in the Ribbon. The Find dialog box opens; type the word or phrase you want to find in the Find what field. Change the Match whole word only and Match case settings if needed; then click **Find Next**. WordPad locates and highlights the first instance of the word or phrase you typed in the Find What field. If necessary, continue clicking **Find Next** until you locate the passage you need. When you are finished searching for text, click the Find dialog box's Close button (☒) to close it.

CONTENTS

8

EXPLORING THE INTERNET AND THE WEB WITH YOUR LAPTOP

The Internet and the World Wide Web have revolutionised how we communicate, conduct business, socialise, get information and learn.

Although many people use the terms "Internet" and "World Wide Web" interchangeably, they are two different things. "Internet" refers to a global system of interconnected computer networks; "World Wide Web" describes the massive storehouse of information that resides on that system of interconnected networks. This information is presented on Web sites, which are collections of Web pages that relate to a particular person, business, government, school or organisation. You access Web pages using a special computer program called a Web "browser".

EXPLORE THE INTERNET AND THE WORLD WIDE WEB

The Internet is a massive network of interconnected computers that spans the globe. The enormous amount of information that resides on this network of interconnected computers is known as the "World Wide Web".

This linked collection of data, composed of text, images and other files, is stored on special computers called Web servers and is presented in the form of Web sites. Web sites are composed of Web pages, which users can access using a special program called a Web browser. Each Web page on the World Wide Web has its own distinct "address", also called a uniform resource locator or URL.

Web Page

Information on the Web is organised into Web pages. A Web page may include text, images, sounds and even videos. There are literally billions of Web pages on the World Wide Web, centred on almost every imaginable topic. These Web pages are created by individuals, businesses, governments and other organisations.

Web Site

A collection of Web pages offered by a particular individual, business, government or other organisation is a Web site. There are many types of Web sites: community Web sites, corporate Web sites, e-commerce Web sites, forums, news Web sites, personal Web sites, social-networking Web sites, Web portals, wiki Web sites and more. You might visit a Web site for a variety of reasons, such as to find information about a particular topic, to socialise, to buy or sell products, to play online games or to attend a distance-learning class. Together, all publicly available Web sites comprise the World Wide Web. Note that some Web sites require users to pay to access their content.

Web Server

Web sites are stored on Web servers. A Web server is simply a computer running special software. Web servers "serve" Web pages to Web browsers, enabling users to browse their contents. More powerful Web servers can be set up to handle heavy traffic, such as thousands of visitors at any point in time.

Web Browser

A Web browser is a type of software program that you use to find, display and interact with pages on the World Wide Web. Examples of Web browsers include Apple Safari, Google Chrome, Mozilla Firefox, Opera and Internet Explorer. (Because Internet Explorer is included with Windows 7, it is the Web browser discussed in this chapter.)

Web Address

Each Web page on the World Wide Web has its own unique Web address, also called a uniform resource locator or URL. Your Web browser uses a Web page's Web address to locate the page. You can type a Web address into the Address bar of your Web browser to display the corresponding Web page. Many Web addresses are fairly intuitive; for example, many company Web sites include the company's name.

URLs in Detail

A URL usually consists of four parts. The first is the scheme name or protocol, such as http for Hypertext Transfer Protocol or ftp for File Transfer Protocol. The second part of the URL is the host name of the computer where the page is located, called the third-level domain. An example is www, for World Wide Web. The third part of the URL is the domain name, such as Amazon or IRS. The fourth part of the URL is the Web site top-level domain, such as .co.uk for a business, .ac.uk for a school or .gov.uk for a government site. For example, a typical URL would be http://www.marilynscakes.co.uk.

Internet Service Providers

To connect to the Internet, you must establish an account with an Internet service provider (ISP), sometimes called an Internet access provider. Examples of Internet service providers include BT, Virgin Media and TalkTalk. In addition to offering customers a connection to the Internet, many Internet service providers also provide customers with e-mail accounts as well as other services, such as space on servers to back up data files. Although you can connect to the Internet using a phone line (called a dial-up connection), this type of connection is very slow and practically obsolete; higher-speed technologies such as DSL and cable are strongly recommended. You can also connect to the Internet through a wireless network or hotspot, often found in airports and hotels.

CONNECT TO THE INTERNET

Before you can use your laptop to access the World Wide Web, you must connect it to the Internet. To do so, you must establish an account with an Internet service provider (ISP) such as BT, Virgin Media or TalkTalk.

Usually, when you obtain an account with a broadband Internet service provider, a technician is sent to your home to set up the Internet connection. If not, you can set up the connection yourself using the Windows 7 Connect to the Internet Wizard.

① Connect the modem (provided by the ISP) to your computer.

Note: *Make sure the modem is also plugged in to a power supply and to the appropriate jack in your wall.*

② Click the **Start** button (⬤).

③ Click **Control Panel**.

The Control Panel window opens.

4 Under the Network and Internet section, click **Connect to the Internet**.

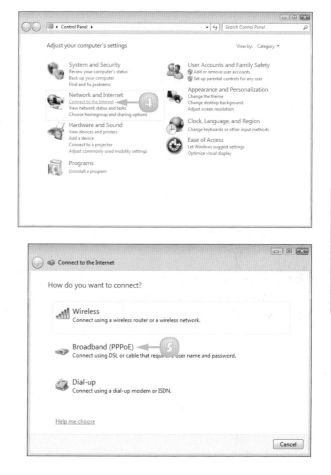

Windows launches the Connect to the Internet Wizard.

5 Follow the on-screen prompts (obtain the username and password from your ISP).

✓ *With a fast Internet connection, data can be sent over the Internet and Web pages can be displayed more quickly. Dial-up connection speeds tend to max out at 56 kilobits per second (Kbps) but most broadband connections average around 500 to 600 Kbps.*

✓ *If your laptop has a wireless card, you may be able to connect to the Internet via a wireless network, or a WiFi connection. Wireless networks are often found in public places such as hotels, libraries and cafes, as well as in homes and businesses. Chapter 11 covers setting up and connecting to a wireless network.*

NAVIGATE THE INTERNET EXPLORER 8 BROWSER

A Web browser is a software application that you use to locate and view Web pages. There are several Web browsers, each providing their own set of features. (Be aware that some Web browsers may display Web page features differently.) Examples of Web browsers include Apple's Safari, Mozilla Firefox, Opera and Microsoft Internet Explorer.

Laptop PCs running Windows 7 come with the latest version of Internet Explorer preinstalled. (As of this writing, the latest version of Internet Explorer is Internet Explorer 8.) You start Internet Explorer by clicking the program's icon in the Start menu or the taskbar.

118

A Navigation Buttons

Click the **Back** (🔙) button to return to the last page you viewed. Click the **Forward** (🔜) button to redisplay the page shown when you clicked the **Back** button.

B Address Bar

Type the Web address of the page you want to visit in the Address bar.

C Refresh and Stop Buttons

Click the **Refresh** button (🔄) to ensure that the page you see contains the most up-to-date information. Click the **Stop** button (❌) stop the page-loading process.

D Search Box

Type a keyword or phrase in the Search box and press **Enter** to find related Web sites and pages.

E Favorites

Click the **Favorites** button to open the Favorites Center, where you can view a list of favorite sites.

F Quick Tabs

Quick Tabs enable you to open multiple Web pages within a single browser window. Each page is displayed in a tab.

G Links

Links often appear as coloured, underlined text. You can click a link to open a new Web page. Buttons and images can also function as links.

H Toolbar

The Windows Explorer 8 toolbar includes buttons for changing the home page (the page displayed by default), e-mailing pages, printing pages, accessing page options and more.

OPEN A WEB PAGE

You can open a Web page in Internet Explorer using a variety of techniques. For example, you can click a link on a Web page to open a new page. Or, if you have recently visited the Web page, you may be able to access it by right-clicking the Internet Explorer button on the taskbar and choosing the page from the list that appears. Otherwise, if you know the page's Web address, you can simply enter it in the Address bar. If you do not know the page's Web address, you can search for the page; see the section "Search the Web" for help.

1 In the Address bar, type the URL of the Web page you want to visit.

A As you type a Web page's address in the Address bar, Internet Explorer displays a list of URLs.

2 If the URL for the page you want to visit appears, you can click it in the list.

3 If the URL does not appear, type it in its entirety and press Enter.

Internet Explorer displays the Web page whose address you entered.

BROWSE WITH QUICK TABS

Suppose you want to use the Internet to compare the price of lodging on various hotel Web sites. In earlier versions of Internet Explorer, you had to open a separate browser window for each site and switch among them, which was often a hassle.

To address this, Microsoft developed a feature called Quick Tabs. With Quick Tabs, you can open multiple Web pages at once within a single browser window, displaying each in its own tab. To switch to a different page, simply click its tab. When you are finished with a page, you can close its tab.

Launch a Page in a New Tab

① Click the blank tab that appears to the right of any populated tabs.

Ⓐ A blank tab opens.

② Type the URL for the page you want to open in the new tab.

The page opens.

Open a Link in a Tab

 Right-click the link whose page you want to view in its own tab.

2 Click **Open Link in New Tab**.

Note: An even faster way to open a link in a new tab is to click the link while pressing and holding **Ctrl**.

A A tab for the new page appears.

Note: This new tab is the same color as the tab containing the link, making it easy to see which open tabs are part of the same group.

3 Click the tab to view the page.

B To close a tab, click its **Close** button (**X**).

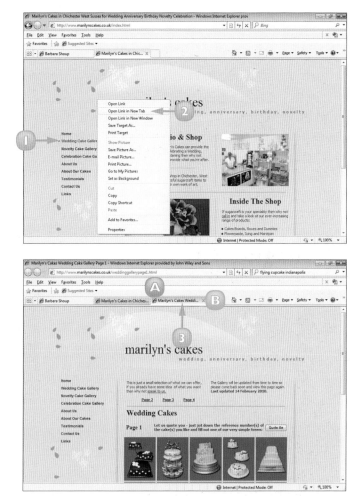

You can also switch tabs by clicking the Quick Tabs button (⊞) to the left of the tabs to view previews of all the pages currently open in your browser window; then click a preview to switch to the corresponding tab. Alternatively, click the ▾ to the right of the Quick Tabs button (⊞) to view a list of all available tabs; then click a tab in the list to open it. A third option is to position your mouse pointer over the Internet Explorer button (🕮) on the taskbar. Previews of each open tab appear; click the desired tab's preview to display it in your browser window.

SEARCH THE WEB

You will often want to perform searches to locate Web pages of interest. You could direct your Web browser to a search engine Web site, such as www.bing.com or www.google.com, but an easier approach is to use the Internet Explorer Search box.

When searching, using more specific keywords or phrases yields more targeted results. For example, instead of simply using the keyword *motorcycle*, try *Ducati Monster 1100 S*. To search for a specific phrase, surround it with quotation marks.

You can also use Internet Explorer to search for a specific word or phrase within an open Web page in your browser window.

Search for a Web Page

1. Type a keyword or phrase in the Internet Explorer window's Search box.

   A. *As you type, Internet Explorer displays a list of suggestions of topics that match your text.*

2. If the topic you are searching for appears in the list, click it.

3. If the topic you want does not appear, type your text in its entirety and press **Enter**.

   Internet Explorer launches Bing, with the results of your search shown in list form.

4. Click a link in the search results list.

   Windows displays the page whose link you clicked.

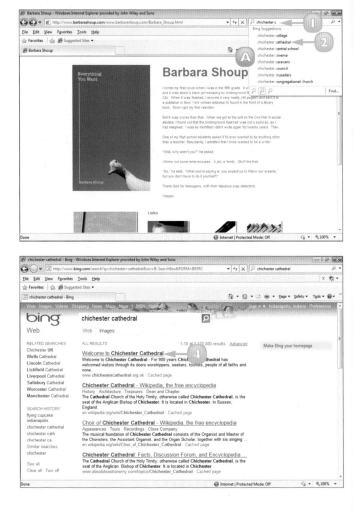

Search for Text in a Web Page

1. Type a keyword or phrase in the Internet Explorer window's Search box.

2. Click the down arrow to the right of the **Search** box.

3. Click **Find on this Page**.

   A. *The Find bar appears, with the text you typed displayed.*

   B. *Internet Explorer highlights matching text on the page.*

4. Click **Next** to locate the next match; click **Previous** to find the previous instance.

   C. *Click the **Options** and click **Match Whole Word Only** or **Match Case** to narrow your search accordingly.*

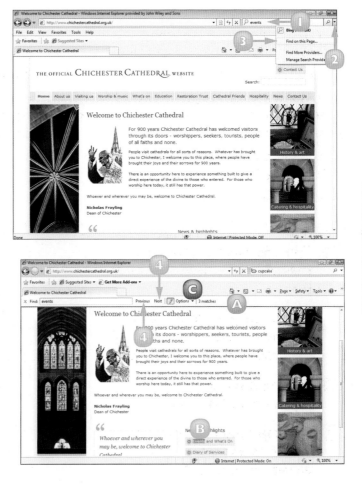

*You can use search tools that provide results relating to shopping, sports, movies, news and more. Click the Search , click **Find More Providers** and click a tool's **Add to Internet Explorer** button in the list that appears. You can click the **Make this my default search provider** check box ( ), then click **Add**. To search using the alternative provider, type a keyword or phrase in the Search box, click the Search and click the name of the provider.*

Boasting literally billions of Web pages, the Internet is without question an incredible resource for information. Its sheer scope, however, can make finding the information you need a chore.

When you do find a page that you know you will want to revisit, you can use Internet Explorer to mark that page as a "favourite". When you do this, Internet Explorer saves it in a special list, called the Favorites list. When you are ready to revisit the page, you can simply click the page's entry in the list.

Save a Page as a Favorite

1. Open the page you want to save as a favourite.

2. Click the **Favorites** button.

   Ⓐ *The Favorites Center opens.*

3. Click **Add to Favorites**.

   The Add a Favorite dialog box opens.

4. Type a name for the favourite.

5. Click ▪ and select the folder in which you want to save the favourite.

6. Alternatively, to save the favourite in a new folder, click **New Folder**.

7. In the Create a Folder dialog box, type a name for the new folder.

8. Click ▪ and select the folder in which you want to save this new folder.

9. Click **Create**.

10. Click **Add**.

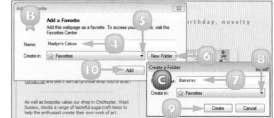

124

The page is added to your list of favourite pages.

Open a Favorite

1. Click the **Favorites** button.

2. If necessary, click the **Favorites** tab.

3. If the page you want to visit has been saved in a folder, click the folder.

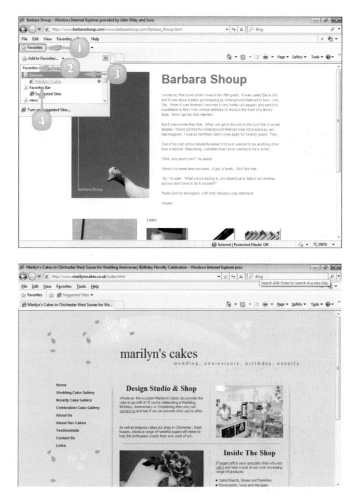

4. Click the page you want to visit.

The page opens and the Favorites Center closes.

Note: *To keep the Favorites Center open, click the **Pin the Favorites Center** button (⬚) before you click the site you want to visit.*

☑ **To delete a favourite, right-click it in the Favorites list and click Delete from the menu that appears. Internet Explorer prompts you to confirm the deletion; click Yes.**

☑ **If you access a page on a daily basis, you might prefer to save it on your Favorites bar, located immediately below the Address bar. To add a favourite to the Favorites bar, you simply open the desired page and click the Add to Favorites Bar button (⬚); a button for the page appears under the Address bar.**

CHANGE YOUR HOME PAGE

If you frequently visit a particular Web page, such as a news site, you can direct Internet Explorer to open that page by default anytime you launch the program or click the browser's Home button. This saves you the trouble of typing the site's URL in the Address bar or selecting the site from your Favorites list.

If you want, you can set multiple home pages – for example, a national news site, a local news site, a stock ticker – to launch automatically at startup or when you click the Home button.

Add a Single Home Page

① With the page you want to set as your home page open in Internet Explorer, click the ▾ to the right of the **Home** button (🏠).

② Click **Add or Change Home Page**.

The Add or Change Home Page dialog box appears.

③ Click the **Use this webpage as your only home page** option button (◉).

④ Click **Yes**.

Windows sets the current page as your home page.

Add Multiple Home Pages

1. With the pages you want to set as your home pages open in Internet Explorer, click the 🔽 to the right of the **Home** button (🏠).

2. Click **Add or Change Home Page**.

    The Add or Change Home Page dialog box appears.

3. Click the **Use the current tab set as your home page** option button.

4. Click **Yes**.

    Windows sets the current tab set as your home page.

Note: *If you no longer want to launch a page at startup, click the 🔽 to the right of the Home button (🏠) and click Remove. Then click the page you no longer want to launch at startup.*

✓ **The History list keeps track of sites you have visited. One way to view your History list is to click the 🔽 on the right side of the Address bar; Internet Explorer displays a list of recently visited Web pages. You can click a page in the list to open it. To view even more pages in your History list, click the Favorites button to open the Favorites Center; then click the History tab. A list of pages you have visited, sorted by date, appears; simply click a page in the list to open it in the browser window.**

CONTENTS

GETTING ORGANISED WITH WINDOWS 7

Windows Live Mail, which you downloaded in Chapter 3, offers simple Contacts and Calendar tools for keeping track of your contacts and appointments. Perhaps a better option, however, is to use the more robust Windows Live Contacts and Windows Live Calendar, covered in this chapter. Both are offered free of charge from Microsoft's Windows Live Web site.

To use these tools, you must set up a Windows Live account. After you do, simply direct your Web browser to the Windows Live Web site (http://home.live.com) and log in.

IMPORT CONTACTS INTO WINDOWS LIVE CONTACTS

Windows Live Contacts stores contact information you enter about people and organisations. But what if you have already entered much of that information in another contacts-management program? Fortunately, instead of requiring you to re-enter that information by hand, Windows Live Contacts enables you to import it. Windows Live Contacts can import contacts from Microsoft Outlook (covered here), Outlook Express, Windows Contacts, Windows Live Hotmail, Yahoo! Mail, Gmail, and more.

Before you can import contact information, you may need to export it from your current program. The precise steps for this differ depending on the type of program you use. For details, see your program's help information.

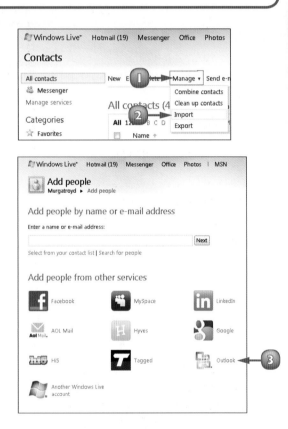

① In the main Windows Live Contacts screen, click **Manage**.

Note: To display the main Windows Live Contacts screen, position your mouse pointer over the **Windows Live** link in the upper-right corner of the main Windows Live screen, click All **Services**, and click **Contacts**.

② Click **Import**.

The Add People screen appears.

③ Under Add People from Other Services, click an e-mail service (here, **Outlook**).

The Import Contacts screen appears.

④ Click the option button next to your old contacts-management program.

⑤ Click **Browse**.

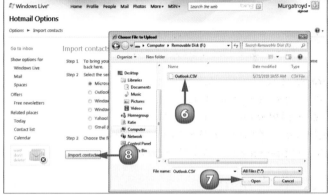

The Choose File to Upload dialog box opens.

⑥ Locate and select the file containing the contacts you want to import.

⑦ Click **Open**.

⑧ Click **Import contacts**.

Windows Live Contacts imports your contacts. To view your contacts, click **Return to contacts**.

By default, contacts are listed alphabetically by first name, but you can sort them by last name if you prefer. To do so, click Options in the upper right corner of the screen, click More Options, and then click Display Contacts As... under Customize Your Contacts. Then click the Last, First option button (⊙) and click Save.

ADD A CONTACT

In addition to importing contacts from other programs, you can add new contacts as needed. When you do, you can include as much or as little information about that contact as you like. For some contacts, including a name and an e-mail address may suffice; for others, you might include additional information, such as the contact's work address, fax number, and so on.

To help manage your contacts, you can organise them into categories. For example, you might put all your contacts from one company in a category. Then, you can quickly view all your contacts from that company as a group.

① In the main Windows Live Contacts screen, click **New**.

Note: *To display the main Windows Live Contacts screen, position your mouse pointer over the* **Windows Live** *link in the upper-right corner of the main Windows Live screen, click All* **Services***, and click* **Contacts***.*

② Under Contact Info, enter the contact's first name, last name, nickname, and birthday.

③ Enter the contact's personal e-mail address, home phone number, personal mobile phone number, and home address.

Under Work Info, type the contact's company, work e-mail address, work phone number, pager number, fax number, and work address.

⑤ Click **Save**.

Windows Live Contacts saves your contact.

✓ *You may need to delete a contact entry. Click the check box next to the contact in the main Windows Live Contacts screen; then click the Delete link. When Windows Live Contacts prompts you to confirm the deletion, click Yes.*

133

FIND AND OPEN A CONTACT ENTRY

Windows Live Contacts organises contacts alphabetically by first name. One way to locate a contact is to simply click a letter along the top of the main Windows Live Contacts screen to reveal all contacts whose first name starts with that letter; then scroll down to locate the contact you want.

If you have a large number of contacts, however, this method can be time consuming. Fortunately, Windows Live Contacts includes a search function to enable you to quickly locate the contact you need.

Once you have located a contact entry, you can easily view and open it.

1 Type the contact's name in the Windows Live Contacts **Search** box and press **Enter**.

A *Windows Live Contacts displays a list of contact entries that match what you typed.*

2 Click the contact you want to view.

Windows Live Contacts opens the contact entry.

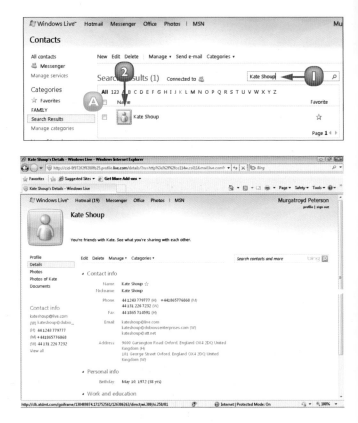

✓ *You can group contacts in categories. Click **Categories** in the main Windows Live Contacts screen and click **New Category**. Type a name for the new category in the Name field and click **Save**. The new category appears in the Manage Categories screen. To add a contact to the category, return to the main Windows Live Contacts screen, click the check box next to the contact you want to categorise, click **Categories**, and click the desired category.*

134

EDIT A CONTACT

You often need to edit contact entries. For example, if someone moves or changes job, you need to edit the Windows Live Contacts contact entry for that person.

When you edit a contact entry, you see the same screen as when you add a new contact. This screen enables you to add or change information such as personal information, business information, and more. As when you add a new contact, you can opt to include as little or as much information as you want when you edit a contact.

 Open the contact entry you want to edit.

Note: *For help opening a contact, refer to the preceding section.*

2 Click **Edit**.

Note: *Alternatively, click the check box next to the contact you want to edit in the main Windows Live Contacts window and then click* ***Edit***.

Windows Live Contacts displays the same screen as when you add a new contact.

3 Click in a field and type over the current contents to update them.

4 When you finish editing the contact information, click **Save**.

Windows Live Contacts saves your changes in the contact entry.

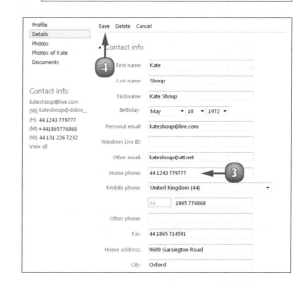

135

ADD AN EVENT TO WINDOWS LIVE CALENDAR

Windows Live Calendar is a great way to keep track of your schedule. Using Windows Live Calendar, you can plan your daily activities by entering appointments, which Windows Live Calendar calls events. These can be one-time events (such as a lunch date with an old friend) or recurring events (such as a standing meeting) that occur on a daily, weekly, monthly, or yearly basis.

By default, Windows Live Calendar sends you a reminder about an event 15 minutes before it starts, although you can direct Windows Live Calendar to send this reminder minutes, hours, or days in advance.

 In the main Windows Live Calendar screen, click **New**.

Note: To display the main Windows Live Calendar screen, position your mouse pointer over the **Windows Live** link in the upper-right corner of the main Windows Live screen, click All **Services**, and click **Calendar**.

 The Add an Event screen appears.

② Type a description of the event in the **What** field.

③ Type the location for the event in the **Where** field.

④ Click **Add more details**.

The Windows Live Calendar Event Details screen appears.

⑤ Click in the leftmost **Start** field and click the date for the event.

⑥ Click in the rightmost **Start** field and click the event's start time.

⑦ Repeat Steps **5** and **6** in the **End** fields to set the end date and time.

⑧ If the event is recurring, click **Set recurrence**.

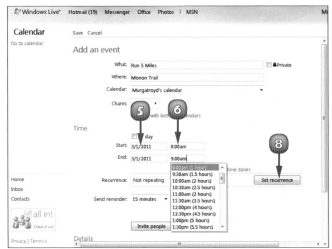

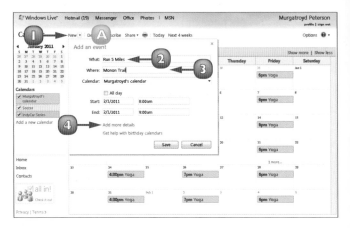

B *The Recurrence section expands.*

9 Click the **Occurs** ⏷ and click **Daily**, **Weekly**, **Monthly** or **Yearly**.

Note: *What you select in Step **9** affects the remaining options in the Recurrence section.*

10 Enter any additional settings in the Recurrence section.

11 Click the **Send reminder** ⏷ and click the number of minutes, hours, or days before the event the reminder should be sent.

12 Click **Save**.

 C *Windows Live Calendar adds the event to your calendar.*

✓ **To invite other people to the event, click Invite people in the Event Details screen. In the To field that appears, type the e-mail addresses for the people you are inviting. When you save the event, Windows Live Calendar asks whether you want to send invitations to the event; if so, click Send.**

✓ **To delete an event – for example, if it is cancelled – position your mouse pointer over the event in Windows Live Calendar and click the Delete Event link. If the event is recurring, you can choose to delete all events in the recurring series or just the selected one. Click Delete to confirm the deletion.**

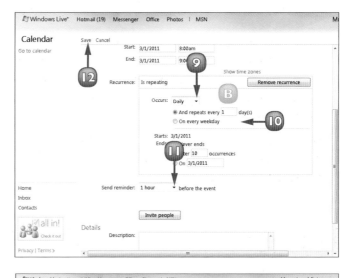

137

CREATE A CALENDAR

Using Windows Live Calendar, you can create multiple calendars. For example, suppose you coach your child's football team and you need to send the upcoming season's game schedule to the other members of the team. Or maybe you need to share your work schedule with your boss so she can keep tabs on you. You can create new calendars – one for the football team, your work schedule, and so on – and add events to them as needed. If you want, you can then share your calendars with others.

1 In the main Windows Live Calendar screen, click the **New** ▼.

Note: *To display the main Windows Live Calendar screen, position your mouse pointer over the* **Windows Live** *link in the upper-right corner of the main Windows Live screen, click* **All Services***, and click* **Calendar***.*

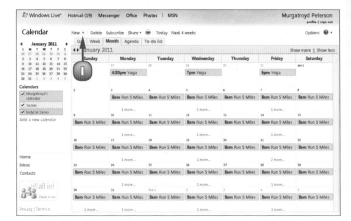

2 Click **Calendar**.

A Alternatively, click **Add a new calendar**.

The Add a New Calendar screen appears.

③ Type a name for the calendar in the **Name** field.

④ Click a colour tile. Events you create for this calendar appear in this colour.

⑤ Type a description.

Ⓑ *If you want to receive a daily e-mail message containing your schedule for the day, click the **Receive a daily e-mail schedule for this calendar** check box (☑) to select it.*

⑥ Click **Save**.

Ⓒ *Windows Live Calendar creates the calendar, listing it with your other calendars. Events in this calendar appear in the colour you chose.*

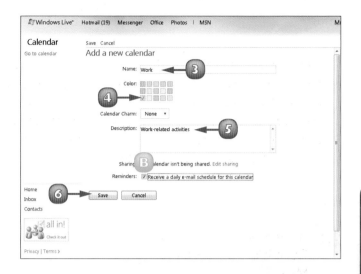

SUBSCRIBE TO A CALENDAR

With Windows Live Calendar, you can subscribe to various public calendars, called iCals. For example, if an iCal exists for your favourite sports team, you can subscribe to it; when you do, entries for each game that team plays appears in Windows Live Calendar.

If you know the URL for the iCal to which you want to subscribe, you can initiate the subscription process from within Windows Live Calendar. Alternatively, you can initiate the subscription process from a calendar portal – that is, a Web site offering access to multiple iCals. One such portal is MarkThisDate.com (www.markthisdate.com).

① In the main Windows Live Calendar screen, click **Subscribe**.

Note: To display the main Windows Live Calendar screen, position your mouse pointer over the **Windows Live** link in the upper-right corner of the main Windows Live screen, click **All Services**, and click **Calendar**.

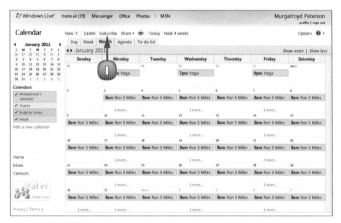

The Import or Subscribe to a Calendar screen appears.

② Click the **Subscribe to a public calendar** option button (◯ changes to ◉).

③ Type the URL for the iCal to which you want to subscribe in the **Calendar URL** field.

④ Type a name for the iCal in the **Calendar name** field.

⑤ Click a colour tile. Events associated with this calendar appear in this colour.

⑥ Click **Subscribe to calendar**.

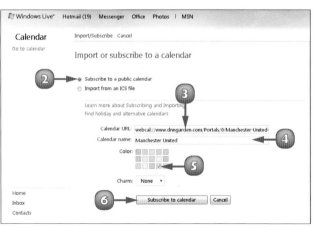

140

Windows Live Calendar informs
you that your subscription was
successful.

⑦ Click **Done**.

Ⓐ *Windows Live Calendar*
subscribes to the calendar,
listing it with your other
calendars.

Ⓑ *Windows Live Calendar adds*
entries contained in the iCal to
your calendar, displayed in the
colour you chose.

☑ **To share your calendars, click**
Share *in the main Windows*
Live Calendar window and
click the calendar you want to
share. The Sharing Settings
screen appears; specify
whether you want to share
your calendar with friends and
family, send friends a view-only
link to your calendar, or make
your calendar public, and then
follow the on-screen prompts.
Finally, click **Save**.

☑ **To stop sharing a calendar,**
click Share *in the main*
Windows Live Calendar screen,
click the calendar you no
longer want to share, select
Don't Share This Calendar,
click **Save**, *and click* **Save**
again to confirm.

CONTENTS

STAYING IN TOUCH

For many, the primary purpose of a laptop is to keep in touch with others – friends, family members and business associates. One way to do this is via e-mail; others are instant messaging (IM) and video chat.

Windows Live Mail is an e-mail program available free of charge from Microsoft's Windows Live Web site. Using Windows Live Mail, you can send, receive, and organise e-mail messages. Windows Live Messenger is a program that you can use to send instant messages and to video chat.

COMPOSE AND SEND AN E-MAIL MESSAGE

You can use Windows Live Mail to compose and send e-mail messages. Before you do, however, you must sign up with an Internet service provider (ISP) and set up an e-mail address either with that provider or with some other source (such as Hotmail). You must also set up your account within Windows Live Mail using the username and password you established with your e-mail provider. For more details on setting up Windows Live Mail, refer to the program's help information. You start Windows Live Mail just as you do any other program in Windows: by clicking the program's icon in the Start menu.

1 Click **New**.

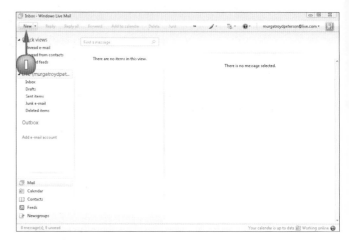

A New Message window opens.

2 Click in the **To** field and type the recipient's e-mail address.

Note: *Windows Live Mail uses Windows Live Contacts as its address book. As you type, Windows Live Mail displays a list of contacts entered in Windows Live Contacts that match what you type. If an entry for the message recipient appears in the list, you can click it to add it to the To field.*

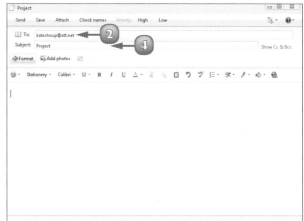

3 Optionally, repeat Step **2** to add more recipients to the To field.

4 Click in the **Subject** field and type a subject for your message.

5 Click in the main message area and type your message.

 6 Click **Send**.

Windows Live Mail sends the message to the contact or contacts listed in the To field.

Note: *If you are not connected to the Internet when you click Send, Windows Live Mail saves your message in the Outbox folder. The next time you are connected, you can send the saved message by clicking the Sync button.*

 A *Windows Live Mail moves a copy of your message to the Sent Items folder.*

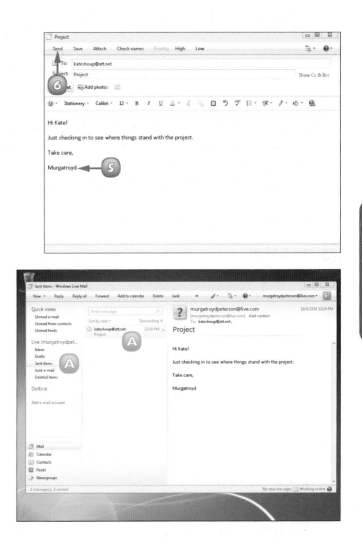

*You should avoid sending e-mail messages when angry. Also, keep things short. Your subject line and the body of your message should be clear, concise, and to the point. Click the **Check Spelling** button (⌨) in the message window's formatting toolbar.*

Windows Live Mail also includes simple Contacts and Calendar tools that synchronise with their more robust online counterparts, Windows Live Contacts and Windows Live Calendar, covered in Chapter 9. You can enter contacts and events from these Windows Live Mail tools or their online equivalents.

ATTACH A FILE TO AN E-MAIL MESSAGE

There may be times when you want to send attachments in your e-mail messages – that is, files you have saved on your computer's hard drive. For example, you might want to e-mail a document containing your CV to apply for a job or you might want to e-mail a PowerPoint presentation to a co-worker for his or her review. When the recipient receives your message containing the attachment, that person can open and view the attached file on his or her computer (provided he or she has the necessary software installed to read the file).

1 In a New Message window, click **Attach**.

A *Windows Live Mail launches an Open dialog box.*

2 Locate and select the file you want to attach.

3 Click **Open**.

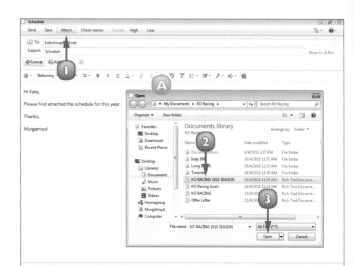

B *An entry for the attached file appears under the message's Subject line.*

SAVE A MESSAGE AS A DRAFT

Suppose you are writing an important e-mail message – for example, a lengthy e-mail about a legal matter or perhaps a personal e-mail sharing the details of a recent vacation with friends – but do not have time to finish it during the current session. If so, you can save the message as a draft. Messages saved in this manner are stored in the Windows Live Mail Drafts folder, one of several predefined folders in Windows Live Mail. When you are ready to work on the e-mail again, you can access it from the Drafts folder.

1 In a New Message window, click **Save**.

A *The Saved Message dialog box opens, indicating where the message has been saved.*

2 Click **OK**.

3 Click the message window's **Close** button ([×]).

4 When you are ready to work on the message again, click the **Drafts** folder.

5 Double-click the message in the File list to open it.

PREVIEW AND OPEN MESSAGES

By default, Windows Live Mail checks for new messages anytime you start the program and at 30-minute intervals, while the program is running (assuming your laptop is connected to the Internet). When you receive an e-mail message, an entry for that message appears in the File list of the Inbox folder, with unread messages appearing in bold. You can preview the message's contents in the Windows Live Mail Preview pane or open it in its own message window. If the message contains an attachment, you can open it directly from Windows Live Mail or save it to your hard drive.

① Click the **Inbox** folder.

Windows Live Mail displays the Inbox folder's File list.

Ⓐ *New messages appear in bold.*

② Click a message in the File list.

Ⓑ *The message's contents appear in the Preview pane.*

③ Double-click the message in the File list.

The message opens in its own window.

Ⓒ *If the e-mail's sender is not in your Windows Live Mail contacts, an Add Contact link appears. Click it to open an Edit Contact dialog box, where you can add info as needed.*

Ⓓ *A paperclip icon indicates that the message contains an attachment — that is, a file appended to the message.*

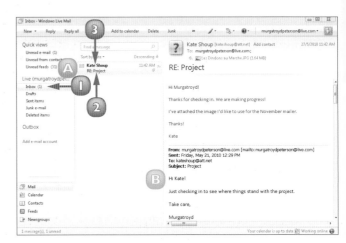

148

Right-click the attachment.

Click **Open**.

Note: To save rather than open an attachment, click **Save As** instead of Open. Windows Live Mail launches the Save Attachment As dialog box; locate and select the folder in which you want to save the attachment and click **Save**.

The file opens.

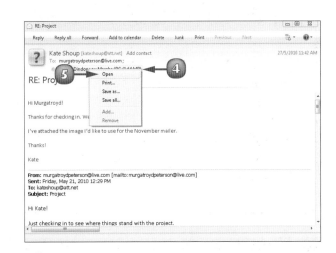

✓ **To check for mail manually, click the Sync ⊡ and click which accounts you want to check. (Click Everything to also sync Windows Live Mail with Windows Live Calendar and Windows Live Contacts.) Windows Live Mail retrieves any new messages and sends any messages currently in the Outbox folder.**

✓ **You can change the time between automatic checks for email. Click the Menus button (⊞) in the Windows Live Mail toolbar and click Options. The Options dialog box opens; in the General tab, make sure the Check for new messages every x minute(s) check box is selected, and enter a number between 1 and 480 in the spin box. Then click OK.**

STOP **Attachments are known carriers of viruses. Open attachments only if they have been sent by a trusted source.**

REPLY TO A MESSAGE

It is not unusual to receive a message for which you want to send a reply. With Windows Live Mail, you can quickly and easily reply to any message you receive.

Sometimes, you will receive messages that were also sent to others. If the message to which you are replying was sent to multiple people, you can reply to the sender only; alternatively, you can choose to reply to the sender as well as to the other recipients.

You can reply to a message from the message window or from the Windows Live Mail Preview pane.

1 Open the message to which you want to reply.

Note: *You can also simply preview the message in the Windows Live Mail Preview pane.*

2 To reply to the sender only, click **Reply**.

A *Alternatively, to reply to the sender and to all other recipients of the original message, click **Reply all**.*

A new message window opens with the original message text.

B *The original subject is preceded with Re:.*

C *The e-mail address of the original sender (and, if you clicked Reply all, the e-mail addresses of the other recipients of the original message) appears in the To field.*

3 Type your reply.

4 Click **Send**.

Windows Live Mail sends your reply.

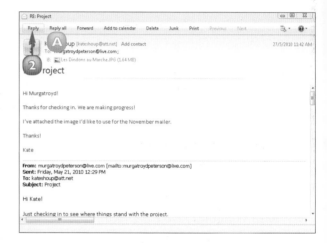

FORWARD A MESSAGE

Often, you will receive e-mail messages that you want to forward to others. For example, you might receive a positive e-mail message from your supervisor that you feel should be shared with other members of your team. Or you might receive an amusing e-mail message from a friend that you want to forward to a mutual acquaintance. Windows Live Mail makes it easy to forward e-mail messages, either from the message window or from the Windows Live Mail Preview pane. You can also add your own text to the forwarded message if desired.

① Open the message you want to forward.

Note: *Alternatively, preview the message in the Windows Live Mail Preview pane.*

② Click **Forward**.

A new message window opens with the original message text.

Ⓐ *The original subject is preceded with **Fw**.*

③ Click in the **To** field and type the recipient's e-mail address.

Note: *As you type, Windows Live Mail displays contacts entered in Windows Live Contacts that match. If the message recipient's name appears in the list, click it to add it to the To field.*

④ Optionally, repeat Step **3** to add more recipients.

⑤ Type any text you want to add to the forwarded message.

⑥ Click **Send**.

Windows Live Mail forwards the message.

SAVE A MESSAGE IN A FOLDER

Suppose you frequently receive e-mail messages from the same person. Or perhaps you receive a large number of messages regarding a project you are working on. If so, you can create a folder for storing those messages and give that folder a descriptive name. Folders you create are added to the Windows Live Mail folder list and appear in alphabetical order. After you create the folder, you can move relevant e-mail messages from your e-mail inbox into that folder, much the way you file papers in file folders to keep them organised.

Create a Folder

1. In the main Windows Live Mail window, click the **New** ▾.

2. Click **Folder** from the menu that appears.

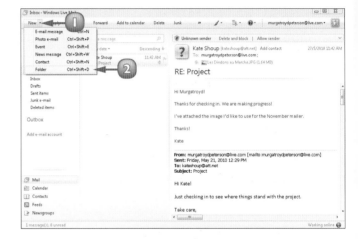

Windows Live Mail launches the Create Folder dialog box.

3. Type a name for the folder in the **Folder name** field.

4. Click the folder in which the new folder should reside.

5. Click **OK**.

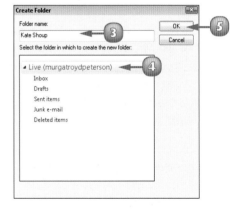

A *Windows Live Mail creates the new folder, placing it in the folder list.*

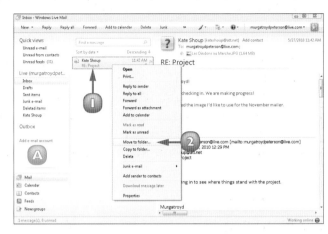

File a Message in a Folder

 Right-click the message you want to file.

 Click **Move to folder**.

Windows Live Mail launches the Move dialog box.

3 Click the folder to which you want to move the message.

4 Click **OK**.

Windows Live Mail moves the message to the folder you choose.

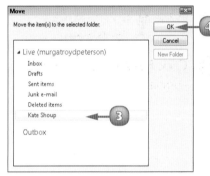

> ✓ *An even faster way to file an e-mail message is to simply drag it from the File list to the folder list, over the folder to which you want to move it. To copy, rather than move, a message to a folder, press and hold* **Ctrl** *as you drag the file to the desired folder.*

> ✓ *To delete a folder, right-click it and click **Delete** from the menu that appears. Windows Live Mail prompts you to confirm the deletion; click **Yes**. Note that when you delete a folder, you delete the e-mail messages within that folder.*

ADD A CONTACT TO WINDOWS LIVE MESSENGER

Windows Live Messenger is an instant-messaging (IM) program that you can download free from the Microsoft Windows Live Web site. You can start Windows Live Messenger by clicking its icon in the Start menu. After you start Windows Live Messenger, you log on using your Windows Live ID.

Before you can communicate with someone using Windows Live Messenger, you must add that person as a Windows Live Messenger contact and invite him or her to chat online with you.

① In the Windows Live Messenger window, click the **Add a Contact or Group** button ().

② Click **Add a contact**.

A Windows Live Messenger dialog box appears.

③ Type the person's IM address in the **Instant messaging address** field.

④ Click **Next**.

5 Type a message to the person you want to invite to chat in the **Include your own message (optional)** field.

6 Click **Send Invitation**.

Windows Live Messenger informs you that you have added the person to your contacts and that, as soon as he or she accepts your invitation, you can chat.

7 Click **Close**.

 You can add a picture to your Windows Live Messenger profile. Click the ▾ next to your screen name and click Change Display Picture. In the dialog box that opens, choose from the available images or click Browse to select an image stored on your hard drive. Then click OK.

RECEIVE AND RESPOND TO AN IM

If Windows Live Messenger is running on your laptop and you are signed in to the service, you can receive IMs in real time from your Windows Live Messenger contacts. When you do, you receive both a visual alert in the taskbar's notification area as well as an auditory alert. When you receive an IM, you can easily respond to it, thereby engaging in a text-based conversation in real time.

A *When you receive an IM, a visual alert appears in the taskbar's notification area.*

1 Click the alert.

B *A Windows Live Messenger window opens.*

2 Type your reply and press **Enter**.

 *To change the sound that plays when someone sends you an IM, right-click the person's name in the Windows Live Messenger window and select **Choose sounds for this contact**. Then, under Sends You an Instant Message, select the sound you want to hear. Finally, click **OK**.*

SHARE A PHOTO

In addition to using Windows Live Messenger to conduct text-based conversations in real time, you can use the service to quickly and easily share a photo at any time in an IM thread. For example, you might share a photo of a new pet, a mutual friend, a funny sign – really, anything. Note that Windows Live Messenger can only support sharing of photos in JPEG, GIF, BMP, or PNG format. When you share a photo with someone else, that person has the option to save it to his or her hard drive.

1 During an IM thread, click **Photos** in the Windows Live Messenger window.

A *A Select Images to Start Sharing dialog box opens.*

2 Locate and select the photo you want to share.

3 Click **Open**.

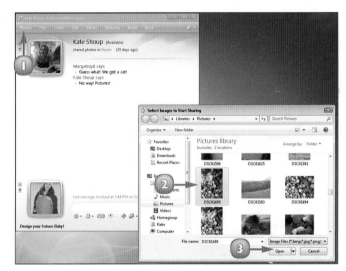

B *The photo is added to the IM thread.*

C *To save a photo in an IM thread, position your mouse pointer over the photo and click the **Save** button (🙂) that appears.*

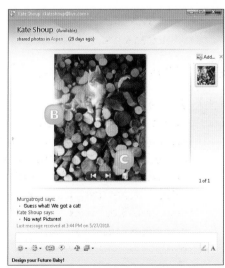

START A NEW IM THREAD

When a contact you have set up in Windows Live Messenger is online, logged in to the service, and available to chat, that person's name appears in your Windows Live Messenger Available list. If you want, you can send that person an instant message, starting a new IM thread.

Windows Live Messenger includes several visual tools for expressing yourself during your IM sessions. For example, you can include emoticons in your messages – small icons that convey a facial expression or other idea. This can help ensure that the true meaning of your message is conveyed.

① Right-click the person you want to IM.

② Click **Send an instant message**.

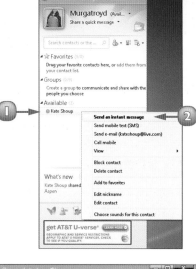

A Windows Live Messenger window opens.

③ Type your message and press Enter.

A The person's reply appears in the Windows Live Messenger window.

4 Type additional IMs as desired.

5 To add an emoticon to an IM, click the **Select an Emoticon** button (☺).

Note: In addition to emoticons, Windows Live Messenger supports winks, which are animated greetings you can send to your contacts, and nudges, which cause the conversation window to vibrate.

6 Click the desired emoticon from the list that appears.

SET UP VIDEO CALLING

In addition to simple text-based conversations, Windows Live Messenger can be used to place video calls. To use Windows Live Messenger for this purpose, your laptop must feature a webcam, a microphone and speakers (a headset is recommended), a broadband Internet connection, and a full-duplex sound card. (With a full-duplex sound card, two people can speak simultaneously.) Also, the person you want to call should be similarly equipped. Note that the quality of the audio and video may vary depending on your hardware and Internet connection speed. Before you can place your first video call, you must set up this feature.

① Click the **Show Menu** button (⊞-).

② Click **Tools**.

③ Click **Audio and video setup**.

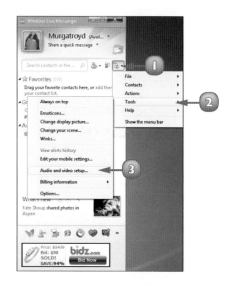

The Set Up Audio and Video – Speaker/Microphone or Speakerphone dialog box opens.

④ Click the **Select the speaker/ microphone or speakerphone you want to use** ▾ and click **Custom**.

⑤ Click the **Speaker** ▾ and click the name of the speaker you want to use.

⑥ Click **Test** to test the speakers. You should hear a series of notes play back.

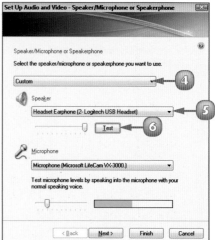

160

Note: When you click the Test button, it toggles to a Stop button. Click **Stop** to stop playing back the series of notes.

 Click the **Microphone** ⏷ and click the microphone you want to use.

 Speak into the microphone.

Ⓐ As you speak, an indicator appears, reflecting the level of your voice.

⑨ Click **Next**.

The Set Up Audio and Video – Webcam dialog box opens.

⑩ Click the **Select the webcam you want to use to place video calls** ⏷ and select the webcam you want to use.

Ⓑ A preview of the webcam feed appears.

⑪ Click **Finish**.

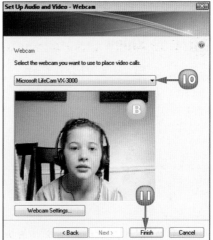

 To adjust webcam settings, click the Webcam Settings button in the Set Up Audio and Video – Webcam dialog box. A Properties dialog box opens, offering settings for adjusting the brightness, contrast, hue, sharpness, exposure, white balance, and more.

PLACE A VIDEO CALL

As mentioned, in addition to using Windows Live Messenger to conduct simple text-based conversations, you can use the service for video calling, assuming your laptop (and the computer of the person with whom you want to speak) has been set up for the job, as covered in the preceding task.

When you place a video call, Windows Live Messenger prompts the call recipient to accept your call. When he or she does, you can commence speaking, and you will be able to see him or her on your laptop screen. You end the call with the simple click of a link.

① Click the **Show Menu** button ().

② Click **Actions**.

③ Click **Video**.

④ Click **Start a Video Call**.

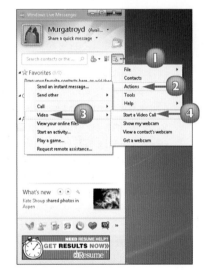

The Select a Contact dialog box opens.

⑤ Click the contact you want to call.

Ⓐ The contact's name appears in the list at the bottom.

⑥ Click **OK**.

Windows Live Messenger starts a video call and invites the selected contact to join in.

B *The feed from your webcam is visible in the Windows Live Messenger screen.*

C *When the recipient accepts the call, the feed from his or her webcam appears in the Windows Live Messenger screen.*

7 Commence speaking as normal.

D *Click and drag the volume slider by your webcam feed to adjust your mic volume.*

E *Click and drag the volume slider by your conversation partner's webcam feed to adjust the speaker volume.*

8 To end the call, click **End call**.

☑ *To switch to full-screen mode, click the* **Switch to Full-Screen View** *button (⬈) next to your conversation partner's Web feed. To revert to regular view, click the* ⬉ *button in the upper right corner of the screen.*

☑ *When someone is attempting to contact you via video call, an alert appears in your taskbar's notification area. Click* **Accept** *or* **Decline**.

CONTENTS

NETWORKING YOUR LAPTOP PC

A network consists of any group of connected computers. Networks enable collaboration through sharing of files, equipment (such as printers) and Internet connections.

There are several types of network. For example, Ethernet networks use special cables to transmit information; HomePNA networks relay data via existing telephone wires; and powerline networks use existing electrical wires to transmit information.

In addition, there are wireless networks, which are the easiest type of network to set up. They also offer laptop users the most mobility because they transmit information via radio waves rather than wires or cables. Using your laptop with a wireless network is the focus of this chapter.

SET UP A WIRELESS NETWORK

Setting up a wireless network is simple – if you have all the necessary components. Specifically, each computer you want to connect to the network needs a wireless card, also called a network adapter. (Most laptops come with wireless cards preinstalled.)

In addition, you need a wireless router, which connects computers and transmits information between them via radio signals. Certain routers are designed to work seamlessly with Windows 7; a feature called Windows Connect Now (WCN) enables you to set them up automatically, as shown here.

Securing your network is critical; otherwise, outsiders may be able to access information shared on your network.

Set Up the Router

1 Plug the router into a power outlet.

Note: You should locate your router such that the computers on your network receive the strongest signal with the least amount of interference. Opt for a central location – as close to the centre of your home or office as possible. Also, position it off the floor and away from walls and from metal objects such as filing cabinets.

2 Click the **Wireless Networks** icon (🔳) in the taskbar's notification area.

A *Windows 7 displays a list of available networks, including an entry for your router (identified by the manufacturer name).*

Note: If your router is not WCN-compliant, use the setup CD that came with the router to set it up manually. For more information, see the Windows 7 Help article titled "Set Up a Wireless Router".

Secure the Router

① Click the **Wireless Networks** icon (🗠) in the taskbar's notification area.

② Click **Open Network and Sharing Center**.

③ Under Change Your Networking Settings, click **Set up a new connection or network**.

✓ *If you want the computers on your wireless network to be able to access the Internet via a shared connection, you need an Internet connection – preferably of the broadband variety (cable or DSL). You obtain an Internet connection and the necessary equipment from an Internet service provider (ISP). To connect your network to the Internet, plug one end of an Ethernet cable into the Internet port on your router and the other end into your broadband modem; then connect the cable supplied by your broadband provider from the appropriate wall outlet to your modem.*

continued →

When securing your wireless network, you should select a passphrase or security key that will be difficult for others to guess, but that you will be sure to remember. Choose a mixture of numbers with uppercase and lowercase letters and avoid strings of characters that compose identifiable words, names or dates. If need be, write down your security key or passphrase and store it in a safe place.

In addition to setting a security key or passphrase, you should install a firewall on each computer on your network to protect the network from hackers and malicious software. You learn how to install a firewall in Chapter 13.

Secure the Router (continued)

Windows 7 launches the Set Up a Connection or Network Wizard.

④ Click **Set up a new network**.

⑤ Click **Next**.

⑥ Click the router you want to configure.

⑦ Click **Next**.

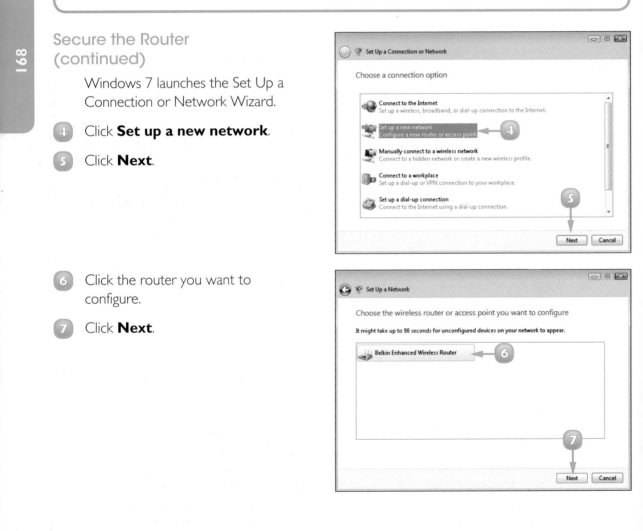

8 Type the router's PIN (located on the bottom of the router).

9 Click **Next**.

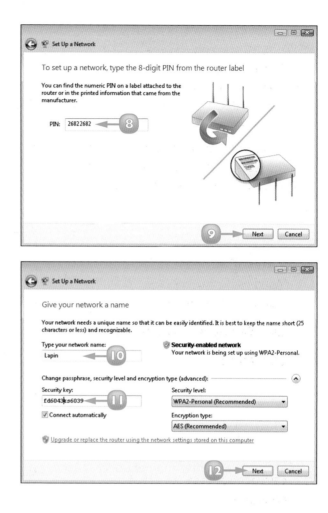

10 Type a name for your network in the **Type your network name** field.

11 Type a security key for your network in the **Security key** field.

Note: *If your network supports the use of WPA2- or WPA-level security, your security key can be a passphrase rather than a cryptic sequence of numbers.*

12 Click **Next**.

Windows 7 applies your changes to the network.

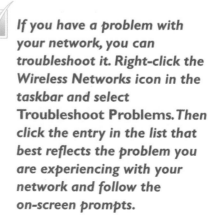

✓ **There are a few different types of wireless network technologies: 802.11a, 802.11b, 802.11g and 802.11n, with 802.11g and 802.11n offering the fastest data-transmission speeds and strongest wireless signals. Your wireless card must be compatible with the network technology that your wireless router uses.**

✓ **If you have a problem with your network, you can troubleshoot it. Right-click the Wireless Networks icon in the taskbar and select Troubleshoot Problems. Then click the entry in the list that best reflects the problem you are experiencing with your network and follow the on-screen prompts.**

CONNECT TO A WIRELESS NETWORK

After you set up your wireless network, you can connect to it with your laptop – assuming your laptop has a wireless card installed.

If your wireless network is connected to the Internet, you can then access the Internet from your laptop. You may also be able to access files that other computers are sharing on the wireless network.

In addition to connecting to your own wireless network, you can connect to public wireless networks, often found in airports, hotels, cafes, libraries and other public places.

① Click the **Wireless Networks** icon (▣) in the Windows 7 taskbar's notification area.

A list of wireless networks in your area appears.

② Click the wireless network you want to use to connect.

Ⓐ A Connect button appears.

③ Click **Connect**.

④ If prompted, enter the network password or network security key.

⑤ Click **OK**.

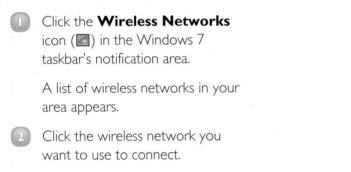

If this is the first time you have connected to this wireless network, Windows 7 prompts you to specify whether it is a home, work or public network.

 **6** Click **Home network**, **Work network** or **Public network**.

Windows 7 confirms your selection.

7 Click **Close**.

Note: *If connecting to a public network, you may need to create an account to log on. To find out, launch your Web browser.*

Note: *To disconnect from a wireless network, click the **Wireless Networks** icon (* ▦ *) in the Windows 7 taskbar, click the wireless network to which you are connected and click* ***Disconnect****.*

✓ **To determine whether your computer features a wireless card, open Windows 7 Device Manager, double-click the Network Adapters entry in the list of devices and look for a device with "wireless" or "WiFi" in its name.**

✓ **You connect to a public network in the same way as a private one, but you may have to create an account with the public network provider to log on. To find out, launch your Web browser after connecting to the network; if an account is required, you will be directed to a special Web page where you can create one.**

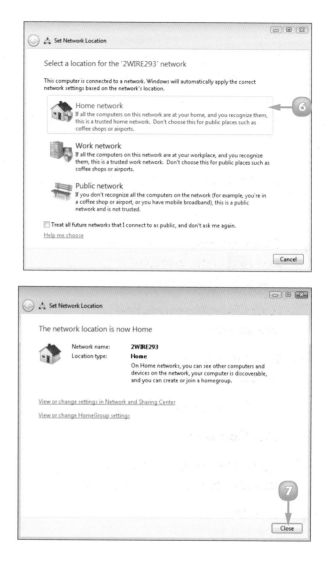

SHARE FILES AND FOLDERS VIA PUBLIC FOLDERS

Windows 7 offers special folders, called Public folders, which you can use to share files and folders with other users. There are four Public folders: Public Documents, Public Music, Public Pictures and Public Videos. These folders are subfolders of the main Documents, Music, Pictures and Videos folders, respectively.

When you place an item in a Public folder, any other person with a user account on that same computer can view it by default. In addition, you can make these folders accessible to other users whose computers are connected to your network. To do so, you must enable sharing.

1 Click the **Wireless Networks** icon (🖳) in the taskbar's notification area.

2 Click **Open Network and Sharing Center**.

The Network and Sharing Center window opens.

3 Click **Change advanced sharing settings** on the left side of the Network and Sharing Center window.

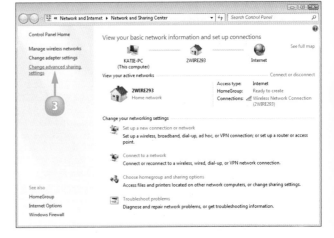

172

The Advanced Sharing Settings window opens.

Note: *An even faster way to open the Advanced Sharing Settings window is to open one of your Public folders, click* **Share With** *and click* **Advanced Sharing Settings***.*

4 If necessary, click the ⊡ to the right of your current profile to expand it.

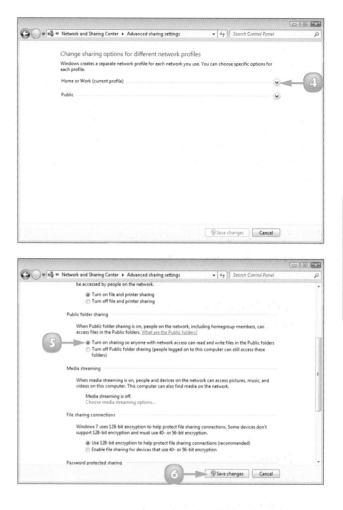

5 Under Public Folder Sharing, click the **Turn on sharing...** option button to select it.

6 Click **Save changes**.

✓ **To share a file or folder, simply move or copy it to the relevant Public folder to make it accessible to others. When you do, others can open and work with the file or folder as if it were stored on their own PC.**

✓ **To limit what others can do with items you share, you can apply permissions. Permissions are rules that specify the level of access a user has. For example, you can limit others to simply opening files you share or you can allow them to modify them or even create new files in your shared folders. For details, see the Windows 7 Help information.**

SET UP A HOMEGROUP

You can share files and folders by creating a homegroup, which other Windows 7 computers on your network can join. When you create or join a group, you specify which of your items you want to share and which should remain private.

To create a homegroup, your network must be a home network (as opposed to a work or public network). To change from a work or public network to a home network, click the Public Network or Work Network link in the Network and Sharing Center window and click Home Network in the screen that appears.

1 In the Network and Sharing Center window, next to HomeGroup, click **Ready to create**.

Note: *To open the Network and Sharing Center window, click the **Wireless Networks** icon (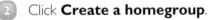) in the taskbar's notification area and click **Open Network and Sharing Center**.*

The Homegroup window opens.

2 Click **Create a homegroup**.

The Create a Homegroup Wizard starts.

③ Click the check box (☑) next to each folder you want to share with the homegroup.

Note: *You can also share a printer with your homegroup.*

④ Click **Next**.

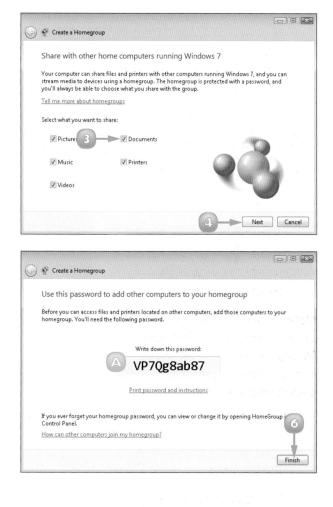

Ⓐ The Create a Homegroup Wizard generates a password.

⑤ Write down the password.

Note: *You need this password to add other PCs to the homegroup.*

⑥ Click **Finish**.

Windows 7 creates the homegroup.

Note: *To add another Windows 7 PC to the homegroup, open the PC's Control Panel and click* **Choose Homegroup and Sharing Options** *under Network and Internet. Click* **Join Now** *in the screen that appears and follow the on-screen prompts.*

Only computers running Windows 7 can join a homegroup. If computers on your network are running a different version of Windows, you must use a workgroup instead. Windows creates a workgroup and gives it a name when you set up a network. To share files and folders among the various computers on the network, you must ensure that the workgroup name listed for each computer is the same. To find out how, view each computer's help information.

CONTENTS

12

MAINTAINING YOUR LAPTOP PC

Periodically performing a bit of housecleaning goes a long way toward keeping your laptop running smoothly. For example, you should regularly ensure that your laptop's Windows 7 operating system has received all the necessary updates from Microsoft, that your files are backed up, that unnecessary files have been deleted in order to free up disk space, that your hard drive is not overly fragmented, that your hard drive is not experiencing errors and that your laptop screen and keyboard are clean and protected. You access many of the tools needed for system maintenance from the Windows 7 Control Panel.

EXPLORE THE WINDOWS 7 CONTROL PANEL

The Windows 7 Control Panel acts like a master console of sorts. It serves as a launching point for performing many system maintenance tasks, such as updating your Windows 7 system, backing up your files, freeing disk space, defragmenting your hard drive and more.

The main Control Panel window features several links. You click a link to access related tools or wizards. If you know the name of the tool you need to access but are not sure which series of links to click to access it, you can use the Control Panel window's Search box to find it.

Click the **Start** button (🔵).

The Start menu opens.

Click **Control Panel**.

178

The main Control Panel window opens.

3 Click **System and Security**.

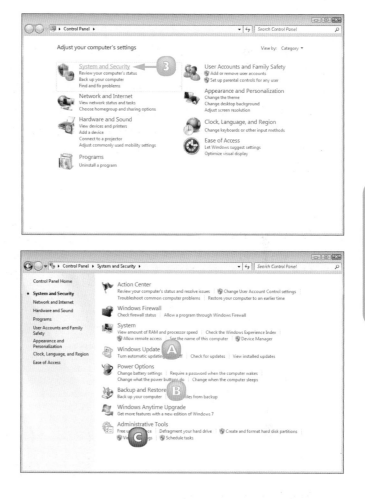

The System and Security window opens.

A Click **Windows Update** to launch the Windows Update tool.

B Click **Backup and Restore** to back up your computer.

C Click **Administrative Tools** to access tools for freeing disk space and defragmenting your hard drive.

If you are not sure what link to click to access a particular tool, you can use the Control Panel window's Search box to find it. Simply type the name of the tool you want to find in the Search box; a list of tools that match what you typed appears.

UPDATE YOUR WINDOWS 7 SYSTEM

Microsoft regularly releases updates for Windows 7 – that is, changes to the operating system designed to prevent or fix problems or to enhance security or performance.

Windows 7 automatically checks for updates and installs those it deems essential. But there are additional, optional updates that Windows 7 does not automatically install; you should regularly view these updates and install them as needed. You can also perform a manual update if Microsoft has released a new update but your system has not yet run its automatic update operation. (Note that to download an update, your laptop must be connected to the Internet.)

① In the Windows Control Panel's System and Security window, click **Windows Update**.

Note: *For help accessing the System and Security window, refer to the section "Explore the Windows 7 Control Panel".*

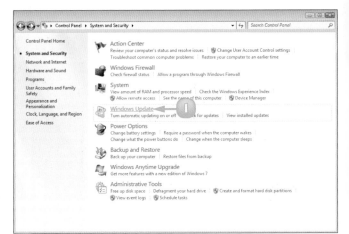

The Windows Update window opens.

Ⓐ *In this case, one important update is available.*

Ⓑ *In this case, two optional updates are available.*

② Click the **X optional updates are available** link.

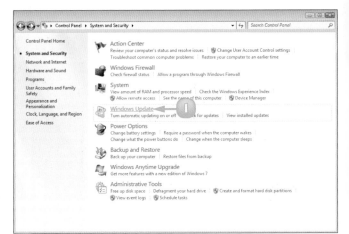

The Select the Updates You Want to Install screen appears.

 3 Click the check box (☑) next to any optional updates you want to install to select them.

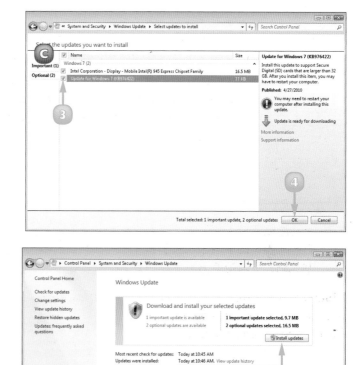

C *You can click **Important** to view the updates Microsoft has deemed essential, which are selected for download by default.*

4 Click **OK**.

5 Click **Install updates**.

Windows 7 downloads and installs any selected updates and informs you when the operation is complete.

Note: *You may be prompted to restart your computer for the updates to take effect.*

*To change the automatic update settings, click **Change settings** on the left side of the Windows Update window. Then, under Important Updates, click the **Install updates automatically (recommended)** ▾ and choose a different option. Click the **Install new updates** ▾ to specify the day and time when updates should run and after reviewing the remaining options, click **OK**.*

SET UP AUTOMATIC BACKUPS

If a disaster such as theft, loss, breakage or virus attack were to befall your computer, certain files, such as digital pictures, would be impossible to replace. Others, such as files used for work, would at best be extremely difficult to reconstruct. For this reason, you should back up your files – that is, copy them to an external hard drive, a Flash drive, a CD, a DVD or a network resource. Wherever you save your backup, you should keep it in a safe, separate location from your computer. You can run manual backups or you can set up Windows 7 to perform backups automatically.

① Connect the drive on which you want to save your backup to your laptop, insert the necessary media or connect to the appropriate network.

Note: *Refer to Chapter 11 for help connecting to a network with your laptop.*

② In the Control Panel's System and Security window, click **Backup and Restore**.

Note: *For help accessing the System and Security window, refer to the section "Explore the Windows 7 Control Panel".*

The Backup and Restore window appears.

③ Click **Set up backup**.

Ⓐ *Windows 7 launches the Set Up Backup Wizard.*

④ Click the drive on which you want to store the backup.

Note: *If your laptop is connected to a network, you may see a Save on a Network button. To save the backup in a folder on the network, click the button and specify the network path and any required username and password.*

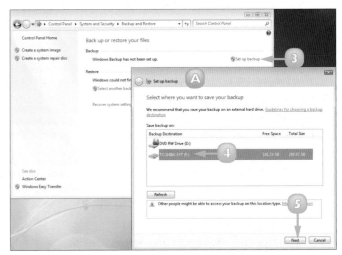

⑤ Click **Next**.

⑥ Click **Let Windows choose** to perform a backup on a standard set of folders.

   🅑 *If you want, you can click **Let me choose** to limit the backup to certain folders.*

⑦ Click **Next**.

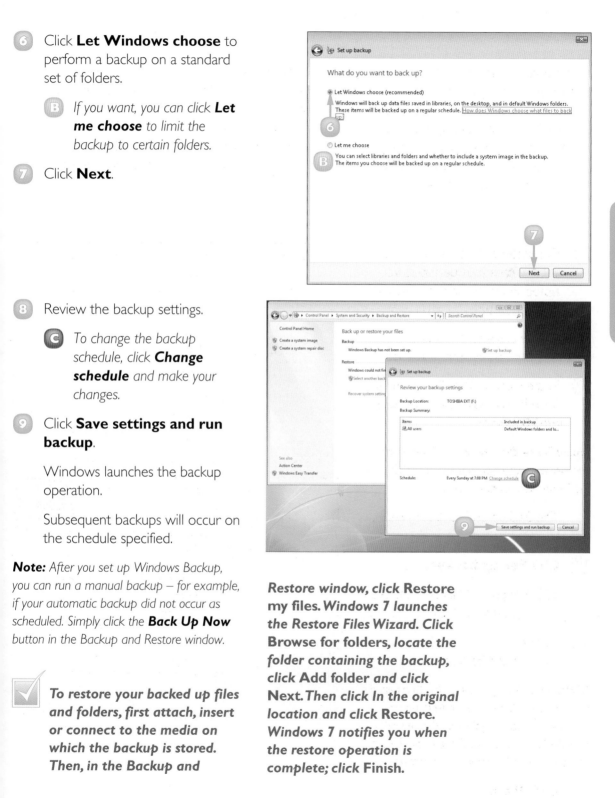

⑧ Review the backup settings.

   🅒 *To change the backup schedule, click **Change schedule** and make your changes.*

⑨ Click **Save settings and run backup**.

Windows launches the backup operation.

Subsequent backups will occur on the schedule specified.

Note: *After you set up Windows Backup, you can run a manual backup – for example, if your automatic backup did not occur as scheduled. Simply click the **Back Up Now** button in the Backup and Restore window.*

✓ **To restore your backed up files and folders, first attach, insert or connect to the media on which the backup is stored. Then, in the Backup and Restore window, click Restore my files. Windows 7 launches the Restore Files Wizard. Click Browse for folders, locate the folder containing the backup, click Add folder and click Next. Then click In the original location and click Restore. Windows 7 notifies you when the restore operation is complete; click Finish.**

DELETE UNNECESSARY FILES

In addition to storing files you create or save as you work on your computer, your laptop's hard drive stores many more files that Windows 7 creates, changes and saves automatically. Over time, you can end up with a gigabyte or more of unneeded files, consuming valuable space on your hard drive.

If your hard drive is low on free space, you can use the Disk Cleanup tool to find and remove these temporary files. This utility also empties the Recycle Bin. In fact, it is wise to run the Disk Cleanup tool regularly as part of standard disk management.

① In the Control Panel's System and Security window, under Administrative Tools, click **Free up disk space**.

Note: *For help accessing the System and Security window, refer to the section "Explore the Windows 7 Control Panel".*

Ⓐ *The Disk Cleanup: Drive Selection dialog box appears.*

② Click the **Drives** 🔽 and select the drive you want to clean.

③ Click **OK**.

Disk Cleanup scans your system to determine how much space can be freed.

184

When the scan is complete, the Disk Cleanup dialog box opens.

④ Click the check box (☑) next to each type of file you want to delete.

⑤ Click **OK**.

Disk Cleanup prompts you to confirm the cleanup operation.

⑥ Click **Delete Files**.

Disk Cleanup deletes the unnecessary files, freeing up disk space.

☑ To quickly view the amount of free space on your hard drive, click the **Start button and click Computer. The Computer** window opens; click the disk you want to check to view the size of the drive and the available space. To view additional information about the drive, right-click its icon and click **Properties**.

☑ To access more details about files that Disk Cleanup wants to delete, click **View Files** in the Disk Cleanup dialog box. These details include the size of the files, when they were created and when you last accessed them.

DEFRAGMENT YOUR HARD DRIVE

When you save a file on your laptop, Windows 7 writes the data to a sector on the hard drive. If the sector is too small to hold the entire file, the extra bits are saved in the next available sector.

Over time, your files may become quite fragmented, with bits spread across several sectors on the drive, meaning that when you open a file, it takes Windows longer to find all the various pieces. To solve this problem, you can run Disk Defragmenter. This reassembles the files on your hard drive such that each one occupies as few sectors as possible.

① In the Control Panel's System and Security window, under Administrative Tools, click **Defragment your hard drive**.

Note: For help accessing the System and Security window, refer to the section "Explore the Windows 7 Control Panel".

Windows 7 launches the Disk Defragmenter utility.

② Click the drive you want to defragment.

Ⓐ Before defragmenting a drive, you can click **Analyze disk** to determine how fragmented it is.

③ To defragment the disk, click **Defragment disk**.

Disk Defragmenter analyzes the disk.

Disk Defragmenter defragments the disk. Note that the process can take several minutes or longer.

Ⓑ *When the operation is complete, the drive is shown as 0% fragmented.*

④ Click **Close**.

You can set up Windows 7 to defragment automatically. Click **Configure schedule** *in the Disk Defragmenter window. Then, in the Disk Defragmenter: Modify Schedule dialog box, select the* **Run on a schedule** *check box and set the frequency with which Disk Defragmenter should run. Next, click* **Select disks**. *Click the disks you want to defragment, click* **OK** *and click* **OK** *again.*

CHECK YOUR HARD DRIVE FOR ERRORS

Problems with your hard drive can cause files to become corrupted. This can prevent you from running a program or opening a document. You can set up Windows 7's Check Disk program to look for and fix hard-drive errors. Then, next time you restart your computer, Windows 7 performs a check.

Check Disk runs two different types of check: a basic hard-drive check and a more thorough bad-sector check. (A bad sector is one that can no longer reliably store data.) You should perform the basic check about once a week and the more thorough bad-sector check once a month.

① Click the **Start** button (⊞).

② Click **Computer**.

The Computer folder window opens.

③ Right-click the disk you want to check.

④ Click **Properties**.

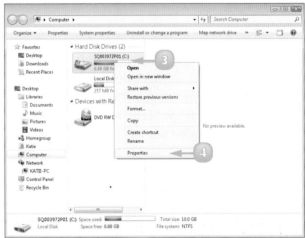

The Properties dialog box opens.

5 Click the **Tools** tab.

6 Click **Check now**.

7 To instruct Check Disk to fix any errors it finds, click the **Automatically fix file system errors** option (☑).

A *To look for bad sectors, check the **Scan for and attempt recovery of bad sectors** option.*

8 Click **Start**.

9 Click **Schedule disk check** to run the check the next time you start your PC.

10 Click the **Start** button (☺).

11 Click the ▶ next to the **Shut down** option.

12 Click **Restart**.

Before restarting your computer, Windows 7 runs the Disk Check utility.

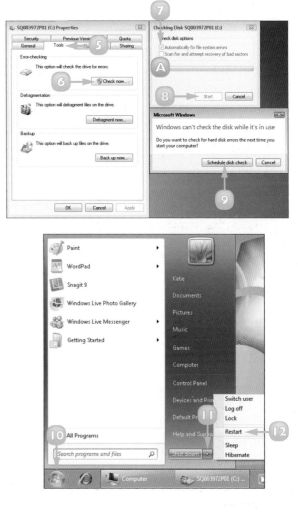

Windows 7 includes a utility called Task Scheduler, which you can use to run tasks automatically. Open the System and Security window in the Control Panel and click Schedule tasks under Administrative Tools. Then create a scheduled task by opening the Action menu and

clicking Create Basic Task. Type a name and description for the task, click Next and specify the schedule on which it should run. Click Start a Program, click Next, click Browse to locate the program you want to launch automatically, click Next again and click Finish.

CLEAN AND PROTECT YOUR SCREEN AND KEYBOARD

Laptop screens are typically of the liquid crystal display (LCD) variety. They are somewhat soft to the touch and can be damaged rather easily. For this reason, you must take care to avoid scratching, poking, denting or puncturing the screen; otherwise, it may become unusable. Although you can replace a laptop screen, doing so is expensive. For this reason, you should take good care of the laptop screen.

You should also take care of your keyboard. It is a good idea to clean your keyboard periodically to keep keys from becoming stuck or damaged.

Clean the Screen

Use a special microfibre cloth (usually made of polyester and nylon) to dust your screen. To avoid denting or otherwise damaging the screen as you clean it, do not press too hard on the screen with the cloth. If you use a liquid cleaning agent, be sure to remove the battery before cleaning your screen.

Cleaning Agents

Avoid ammonia-based household cleaning liquids. These can damage your screen by removing anti-glare and anti-static coatings on the surface. Instead, use isopropyl alcohol. Do not ever spray or pour a cleaner on the monitor surface; instead, coat a cloth or cotton swab with the cleaner and rub that gently on the screen.

Protect Your Screen from Damage

When you are not using your laptop, close the clamshell lid. Consider purchasing a padded bag for your laptop for storing when not in use. Never place sharp objects, such as pens or your fingernail, against the screen. Be aware that exposure to extreme temperatures can cause problems with laptop displays.

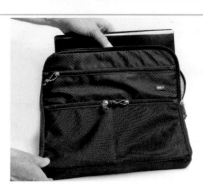

Avoid Spills

To avoid damaging your laptop, it is a good idea to avoid eating or drinking around your laptop. You can clean out spilled crumbs of food, but spilled liquids can be disastrous – especially to your keyboard. If you must eat while working on your laptop, try to keep any liquids at a safe distance.

Clean the Keys

You can clean the keys in a few ways. One is to run a hand-held mini vacuum along the keys to pick up any dust or crumbs that have fallen in. You can also use a nonabrasive liquid cleaner to clean the surface of the keys. Never apply the cleaner to the actual keyboard, however; instead, spray it on a soft cloth and then wipe the keys with the cloth.

Clean Under the Keys

With some keyboards, you can easily remove the keys by gently popping them off with a screwdriver or coin. You can then use a nonabrasive liquid cleaner to clean underneath them. Again, do not apply the cleaner directly; instead, spray it on a soft cloth and then use the cloth to clean under the keys. When you are finished cleaning under the keys, you can simply pop the keys back into place.

Replace a Damaged Key

If you break or otherwise damage a key, you may be able to replace it. Laptop keys are made of three components: the key cap, which is the visible portion of the key; a cup, which is a small rubber component and a hinge, also called a retainer clip. You need all three pieces for the key to function properly. Be aware that removing and replacing larger keys such as the spacebar is slightly more difficult. You should check your owner's manual first to see if your manufacturer recommends replacing a key.

CONTENTS

SECURING YOUR LAPTOP PC

If your laptop is connected to the Internet, it is vulnerable to any number of threats, including crackers, viruses, spyware and more. Even an unconnected laptop can be compromised by someone who gains physical access to it.

Fortunately, you can take certain steps to counter these threats. For example, password-protecting your laptop prevents someone who gains physical access to it from logging on. In addition, you can encrypt your data, install a firewall and filter spam and scams from your e-mail.

You can protect any children who use your laptop by enabling Windows 7 parental controls and Internet Explorer 8's Content Advisor tool.

UNDERSTAND COMPUTER SECURITY

Using your laptop, especially online, gives you access to a great deal of information. That access, however, comes with a price: vulnerability to crackers, viruses, spyware and so on.

One of the best ways to protect yourself is to modify your own behaviour. Just as you would not give personal information to a stranger on the street, you must learn to protect your identity and information online.

In addition, tools are available to help you make your laptop secure. For example, you can set a password, install firewall software or an antivirus program and so on.

Crackers

Crackers are constantly developing new ways to exploit the Internet for ill gain. Some crackers create viruses, which are programs designed with some malicious intent; others use keystroke-tracking software to follow you around online; still others gather information that you contribute to blogs or social sites to steal your identity. Note that crackers should not be confused with hackers. Where crackers exploit technology for ill gain, hackers simply enjoy the challenge involved in breaking into computer systems. Unlike crackers, hackers do no harm. In fact, true hackers subscribe to a strict code of ethics and frown upon crackers.

Viruses

A virus is a program created with malicious intent to copy itself and infect computers. Many viruses are distributed via e-mail, although some are downloaded alongside other files. Viruses can have a range of effects, from destroying data on your hard drive, to making changes in your operating system to open up a security gap, to making copies of a file until your laptop's memory is overwhelmed. Although the term *virus* is sometimes used to refer to other types of hostile, intrusive or annoying software or code such as worms, Trojan horses, spyware and so on, only self-replicating programs can truly be called viruses.

Spyware

Spyware is a type of malicious software or *malware*, that attaches to other software that you download and installs itself on your computer. Spyware can take control of your laptop without your knowledge, collecting little bits of information about you as you work. For example, spyware might collect personal information that you would prefer to keep private, such as your Internet surfing habits. More than that, though, spyware can perform such nefarious tasks as redirecting your browser to a bogus Internet site, where you might be prompted to enter personal information or installing unwanted software on your laptop. Spyware may also result in unwanted pop-up ads appearing on your laptop.

Behaviour

When using your laptop to surf the Internet, be careful where you go. Just as you do not walk in the worst part of town at midnight, so, too, you should avoid the unsavoury parts of the Web. If you choose to register with a site and provide personal information, make sure that the site is secure and that they do not make your information public. Submit information or purchase items online only at sites that you trust. Do not post personal information on a public blog or other site. Information about your location, your family, your income or your activities can provide what a predator needs to locate, stalk or rob you.

Password

You can set up your laptop to require a password to log in. By setting a password, you prevent others who do not know your password from logging in to your Windows 7 laptop and accessing your files. Be sure to set a strong password to prevent others from cracking it. Your password should be at least eight characters long, should be a mixture of uppercase and lowercase letters and should not contain your username, your real name, your company's name or any complete words. Also, it is a good idea to periodically change your password. If you are worried you will forget your password, you can write it down, but be sure to store the written password somewhere safe and private.

Firewall

A firewall is a software program that stops certain types of data from passing from the Internet to your laptop (and vice versa) while still allowing other types of data to pass through. All data travelling between your laptop and the Internet passes through the firewall; the firewall examines each piece of data to determine whether it should be allowed to pass, blocking any data that does not meet the specified security criteria. A firewall is meant to help prevent intruders from accessing the data on your laptop via the Internet. Windows 7 includes its own firewall, called Windows Firewall, for use on your laptop.

Antivirus Software

Antivirus software, such as Norton AntiVirus, McAfee and the free Microsoft Security Essentials, can be installed and set up to run regular scans for malware, including viruses, worms and Trojan horses. Some antivirus software is also designed to scan for spyware and adware. (Adware is software installed on a computer, usually without the user's knowledge, that automatically displays advertisements.) Be sure to regularly run the Update Virus Definitions feature, because new viruses appear all the time. Keep in mind that antivirus and antispyware programs use system resources, which may be a reason to buy a laptop with extra RAM and CPU processing speed.

PASSWORD-PROTECT YOUR LAPTOP

If you care about keeping your files private, creating a password is crucial. Doing so prevents anyone who does not know the password from logging on to your account and accessing your files.

Setting a strong password is important – that is, is the password should be at least eight characters long; should not contain your username, your real name, your company's name or any complete words; and should contain a mixture of uppercase and lowercase letters, numbers, symbols and spaces. For an added layer of protection, consider changing your password periodically. If you write down your password, be sure to store it somewhere safe and private.

1 In the main Control Panel window, click **User Accounts and Family Safety**.

Note: *To open the Control Panel window, click the* **Start** *button (*▦*) and click* **Control Panel**.

The User Accounts and Family Safety window opens.

2 Under User Accounts, click **Change your Windows password**.

The User Accounts screen opens.

3 Click **Create a password for your account**.

4 Type the password you want to use in the topmost field.

5 Type the password a second time in the next field to confirm it.

6 Type a password hint in the next field.

Note: *If you forget your password, press* `Enter` *when Windows 7 displays the Welcome screen to view your password hint.*

7 Click **Create password**.

Windows 7 password-protects the user account.

✓ *You can set Windows to require a password when your laptop "wakes" from Sleep mode.* *Click* **Hardware and Sound** *in the Control Panel window; then, under Power Options, click* **Require a password on wakeup.** *The System Settings screen appears; select the* **Require a Password** *option button and click* **Save changes.**

✓ *If you forget your password, the administrator must reset it. If you forget the password for an Administrator account and no other Administrator accounts are on the laptop, you must reinstall Windows, which means you will lose all your files.*

ENCRYPT YOUR DATA

If someone gains access to your files via a network, you can prevent that person from viewing their contents by encrypting them.

You can use the Windows 7 Encrypting File System, or EFS, to encrypt any files or folders that you store on your drive. With EFS, you choose what files and folders you want to encrypt. When you encrypt an entire folder, you automatically encrypt all of the files and subfolders within it. EFS works by issuing a file encryption key, which EFS then uses to encrypt and decrypt your data.

Note that to run EFS, your laptop must be running Windows 7 Professional, Enterprise or Ultimate Edition.

① In Windows Explorer, right-click the file or folder you want to encrypt.

② Click **Properties**.

Note: *Not all files and folders can be encrypted. For example, compressed files or folders and system files that support your operating system cannot be encrypted.*

The file or folder's Properties dialog box opens.

③ If necessary, click the **General** tab.

④ Click **Advanced**.

198

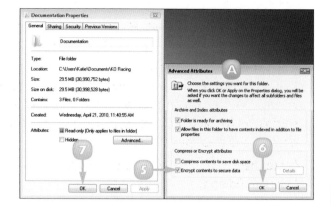

A *The Advanced Attributes dialog box opens.*

5 Click the **Encrypt contents to secure data** check box (☑) to select it.

6 Click **OK**.

7 Click **OK**.

If you are encrypting a folder, the Confirm Attribute Changes dialog box opens, asking whether the encryption should be applied to the folder only or to subfolders and files in the folder.

If you are encrypting a file, the Encryption Warning dialog box opens, asking if you want to encrypt the file and its parent folder or just the file.

8 Select the desired option.

9 Click **OK**.

☑ *If your encryption key is deleted or corrupted, your data will be impossible to recover. It is critical that you back up your encryption key; store the backup on removable media such as a USB flash drive, a CD or DVD or an external hard drive; and keep this media in a safe place. You can also create a recovery certificate. For help backing up your encryption key and creating a recovery certificate, see the Windows 7 Help.*

THWART INTRUDERS WITH WINDOWS FIREWALL

If your laptop is connected to the Internet, it is vulnerable to such dangers as crackers, Internet worms and more. To protect your system, you can enable Windows Firewall, which creates a barrier between your private computer files and outside connections.

When you enable Windows Firewall, it monitors all programs that access the Internet from your computer or try to communicate with you from an external source and moves to block programs that may compromise the security of your system. When this happens, Windows Firewall displays a message asking what you want to do; you can choose to either continue blocking the software or stop blocking it.

Enable Windows Firewall

① In the main Control Panel window, click **System and Security**.

Note: To open the Control Panel window, click the **Start** button (⊞) and click **Control Panel**.

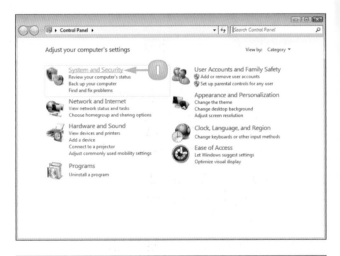

The System and Security window opens.

② Click **Windows Firewall**.

200

The Windows Firewall window opens.

③ Click **Turn Windows Firewall on or off**.

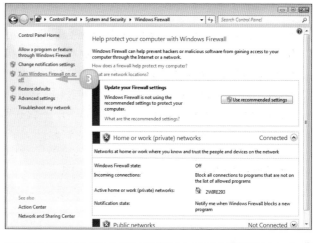

The Customize Settings screen appears.

④ Under Home or Work (Private) Network Location Settings, select the **Turn on Windows Firewall** option button (⦿).

⑤ Make sure the **Block all incoming connections** check box is unchecked.

⑥ Make sure the **Notify me when Windows Firewall blocks a new program** check box is checked.

⑦ Repeat Steps **4**, **5** and **6** under Public Network Location Settings.

⑧ Click **OK**.

Windows 7 enables Windows Firewall.

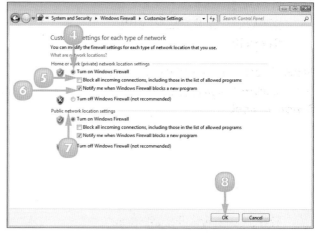

Because they are small and portable, laptops are especially vulnerable to physical threats such as theft as well as prying eyes. Various tools can protect

your laptop from these threats. For example, you can install a fingerprint reader and use your finger, rather than a password, to gain access to your system. To prevent theft, you can buy a cable lock and use it to lock your laptop to a stationary object such as a chair. Another option is to install tracking software to help you track your lost or stolen laptop.

continued ➡

Sometimes, Windows Firewall works a little *too* well. That is, it blocks a safe program or connection. For example, the firewall may block the short-term connection made when you attempt to instant-message with someone.

One way to deal with this is to temporarily disable the firewall. Doing so increases your system's exposure to various security threats, however. A better approach is to allow the problematic network connection or program as an exception. An *exception* is a program or connection that you want to allow so that it does not limit your ability to work or communicate.

Manage Exceptions

1 In the main Control Panel window, click **System and Security**.

Note: *To open the Control Panel window, click the* **Start** *button (*🔵*) and click* **Control Panel**.

2 In the System and Security window, under Windows Firewall, click **Allow a program through Windows Firewall**.

The Allow Programs to Communicate Through Windows Firewall screen appears.

③ Click **Change settings**.

④ Select a program's or feature's check box in the **Allowed programs and features** window to allow it.

Note: *To block rather than allow a program or feature, uncheck the check box next to the program or feature you want to block.*

⑤ Select or deselect the program's or feature's **Home/Work (Private)** and **Public** check boxes to indicate whether the program or feature should be allowed on both types of networks.

⑥ Click **OK**.

You should run antivirus software and be careful when opening files from any source, even a trusted one, to avoid inadvertently infecting your system. Norton and McAfee are two companies that sell reliable antivirus software.

Windows Defender is a program that runs automatically to scan for and uninstall spyware. Spyware is software installed on your computer, usually without your knowledge or consent, that can deluge your system with unwanted pop-up ads and also monitor and record your Web-surfing activities and transmit this data to interested parties – including crackers.

ENABLE WINDOWS 7 PARENTAL CONTROLS

If you share your laptop with children, you can set up the Windows 7 parental controls.

One way to use parental control is to limit children's use of the laptop to certain hours of the day on certain days of the week. If the child tries to log in at a restricted time, Windows 7 blocks access; if the child is logged on at the commencement of the blocked time, Windows 7 automatically logs him or her off.

You can also use Windows 7 parental controls to restrict access to games and other programs on the computer. Games can be restricted by game rating or on a game-by-game basis.

To implement the Windows 7 parental controls, each child who uses your computer must have his or her own Standard user account.

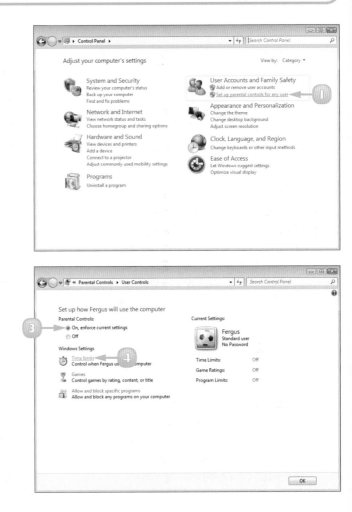

1 In the main Control Panel window, under User Accounts and Family Safety, click **Set up parental controls for any user**.

Note: *To open the Control Panel window, click the* **Start** *button (* 🔲 *) and click* **Control Panel**.

The Parental Controls window opens.

2 Click the user account to which you want to apply parental controls.

The User Controls window opens.

3 Under Parental Controls, click the **On, enforce current settings** option button to select it.

4 Click **Time limits**.

The Time Restrictions window opens.

⑤ Click and drag to indicate the hours during which you want to block or allow computer use for this account.

⑥ Click **OK**.

⑦ In the User Controls window, click **Games**.

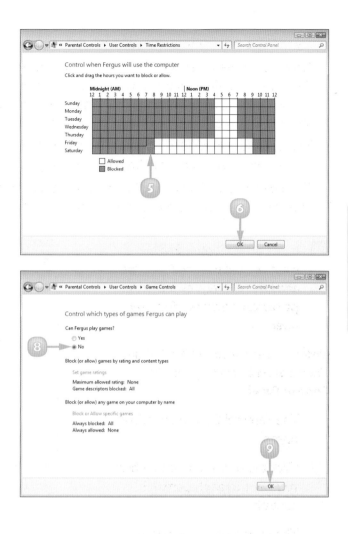

The Game Controls window opens.

⑧ Under Can X Play Games?, click the **No** option (◉ changes to ◉) to prevent the user from playing any games.

Note: To allow the user to play certain games, click **Yes** in Step 8. Then click the **Set Game Ratings** link to block or allow games based on rating. If you want to block certain games, click the **Block or Allow Specific Games** link; The Game Overrides window appears, enabling you to specify which games should be blocked or allowed.

⑨ Click **OK**.

In the User Controls window, you can click Allow and block specific programs and control access to programs in the same way as to games.

You can also use parental controls included with Internet Explorer 8 to prevent exposure to inappropriate subject matter, such as violent or sexually explicit Internet content. Click the Tools button in Internet Explorer 8 and click Internet Options. Click the Content tab and, under Content Advisor, click Enable. The Content Advisor dialog box opens; adjust the settings and click OK.

FILTER SPAM AND SCAMS

In addition to being a real time-waster, spam e-mails often involve scams, making spam potentially dangerous. You can use Windows Live Mail's junk e-mail filter to divert spam from your inbox into a special Junk e-mail folder. The Windows Live Mail junk e-mail filter is enabled by default, but moves only the most obvious junk e-mail messages into your Junk e-mail folder. If you want, you can change the level of filtering.

You should occasionally check your Junk e-mail folder to make sure no legitimate messages were diverted there by accident. E-mails that are not junk can be moved to your inbox.

Change the Filter Level

① In Windows Live Mail, click the **Menus** button ().

② Click **Safety options**.

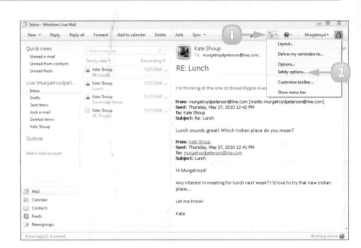

The Safety Options dialog box opens with the Options tab displayed.

③ Select the desired level of protection.

Ⓐ Click **No Automatic Filtering** if you do not want to block any junk e-mail messages.

Ⓑ Click **Low** to block only the most obvious spam.

Ⓒ To block yet more suspected spam, click **High**.

Ⓓ Click **Safe List Only** to block all messages except those from people or domains on your Safe Senders list.

④ Click **OK**.

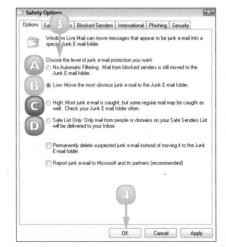

Mark Mail as Not Junk

① Click the **Junk e-mail** folder in the Windows Live folder list.

Ⓐ Messages diverted to the Junk e-mail folder appear in the File list.

② Right-click a message that is not junk.

③ Click **Junk e-mail**.

④ Click **Mark as not junk**.

The message is moved to your inbox.

Note: To ensure that messages from a sender are not blocked, right-click a message from that sender, click **Junk e-mail**, click **Add sender to safe senders list** and click **OK**.

Note: To automatically divert all messages from a sender to your Junk e-mail folder, right-click a message from the sender, click **Junk e-mail**, click **Add sender to blocked senders list** and click **OK**.

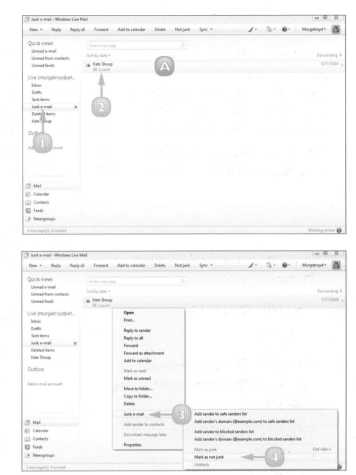

 Phishing is an attempt by a malicious party to obtain private information from computer users. Often, phishing involves an e-mail message that appears to be from a legitimate source, such as a bank, that contains links that direct users to a bogus Web site designed to steal personal information. If you use a Windows Live or Hotmail account with Windows Live Mail, the program automatically checks the sender ID of all incoming messages in an attempt to detect phishing messages. In addition, the Internet Explorer 8 SmartScreen Filter, enabled by default, helps detect fraudulent Web sites.

INDEX